Tea Time

Tea Time

Delicious Recipes, Fascinating Facts, Secrets of Tea Preparation, and More

By Francis Amalfi

Translated by Elizabeth Watson

Skyhorse Publishing

ORIGINAL TITLE: TODOS LOS TÉS DEL MUNDO

© Editorial Océano, S.L. (Barcelona, Spain)

English translation © 2015 by Skyhorse Publishing

Skyhorse Publishing books may be purchased in bulk at special discounts for sales promotion, corporate gifts, fund-raising, or educational purposes. Special editions can also be created to specifications. For details, contact the Special Sales Department, Skyhorse Publishing, 307 West 36th Street, 11th Floor, New York, NY 10018 or info@skyhorsepublishing.com.

Skyhorse® and Skyhorse Publishing® are registered trademarks of Skyhorse Publishing, Inc.®, a Delaware corporation.

Visit our website at www.skyhorsepublishing.com.

10 9 8 7 6 5 4 3 2 1

Library of Congress Cataloging-in-Publication Data is available on file.

Photographs: Becky Lawton, M&G Studios, Rosa Castells-CCL, Cristina Reche, stock photos, Age, Highres, Oceano Ambar Archive
Thanks: Nazanin Amirian, Adriana Ortemberg, Merce Esteve, Dr. Ramon Rosello,
Ed. La Liebre de Marzo, Tea Shop of East West Company
Editing: Montse Vilarnau, Monica Campos, Esther Sanz, Rodolfo Roman
Design editing: Jose Gonzalez

Cover design by Laura Klynstra
Cover photo credit courtesy of Editorial Océano

ISBN: 978-1-63450-343-3
Ebook ISBN 978-1-63450-901-5
Printed in China

Contents

Introduction

*"An after-dinner conversation
without tea disturbs the order of the universe."*

RUDYARD KIPLING

Tea is a legendary drink that continues to gain fans around the world. In fact, its popularity has grown so much in the last two thousand years that today the only beverage consumed more is water.

Someone [Okakura Kakuzō] said that tea "has not the arrogance of wine, the self-consciousness of coffee, nor the simpering innocence of cocoa." Whether used in an infusion, a smoothie, or in cooking, the delicious and delicate flavor of this plant can surprise even the most demanding gourmet.

This treasure of health and flavor was zealously guarded by emperors for many centuries until intrepid merchants from Holland and Britain began to import it to the West.

There are many varieties of tea, defined by their origin and processing, but among all of them, green and white teas stand out for their prodigious health benefits. Their powerful antioxidant effects—and gentle stimulating properties—have been linked to the exceptional longevity of the populations in regions of China and Japan.

This book details all of these benefits and offers delicious recipes for tea lovers to enjoy new flavors in many forms: infusions, cocktails, ice creams, and sauces based on tea.

But just as the universe of *Camellia sinensis*—its botanical name—is immensely rich and varied, in this book we will also see other fascinating aspects of tea culture: the Japanese tea ceremony, a selection of stories for teatime, and even tea leaf readings.

This book also contains a dictionary for connoisseurs, together with an anthology of quotations about this mythical plant from great characters throughout the ages. As Lu Tung said, more than twelve centuries ago, in his celebrated treatise on tea:

Lu Tung, "Song of Tea"

The first cup moistens my lips and throat.

The second cup breaks my loneliness.

The third cup searches my barren entrail, but to find therein some thousand volumes of odd ideographs.

The fourth cup raises a slight perspiration; all the wrongs of life pass out through my pores.

At the fifth cup I am purified.

The sixth cup calls me to the realms of the immortals.

The seventh cup–ah, but I could take no more!

I only feel the breath of the cool wind that raises in my sleeves.

Where is Paradise? Let me ride on this sweet breeze and waft away thither.

Tea culture

The history of tea

A legendary origin

The first documents that mention tea date back to the period between the seventh and sixth centuries BC. The inhabitants of ancient China in this period sang of the excellence of *Tu*, the name given to the group of plants among which we now know as tea. This is the official origin, although if we give credit to popular legend, tea has been around since approximately the year 2700 BC. Between the years 206 BC and

Emperor Chen Nung

The French writer Maxence Fermine describes, in his novel *Opium*, the discovery of tea in China: "One day, more than four thousand years ago, the emperor Chen Nung was travelling with his guard through a distant region of his great country. As the journey was long and tiring, he ordered them to let him stop to rest in the shade of some trees to protect them from the sun. The convoy stopped and the emperor sat cross-legged under an unknown bush. Immediately, he asked for a bowl of boiling water, as he was thirsty and it was the best remedy he knew to quench his thirst. His servants hurried to bring it to him. In that moment, a leaf fell into the emperor's bowl. Chen Nung drank the water without noticing, and when he did a sweet yet bitter aroma filled his throat. Intrigued, he looked into the bowl and found the leaf that gave this fascinating scent and flavor. And thus tea was born."

221 AD, during the Han dynasty, improved methods of gathering and preparing tea leaves made tea a popular beverage of the royal family. Its prestige among the nobility grew, reaching its peak in the period of the Three Kingdoms (221–277 AD), when tea served as a substitute for wine at the court's banquets.

The general population would wait another five centuries before experiencing the goodness of this virtuous plant, since it wasn't until the Tang dynasty, from 618 to 907 AD, that tea became the national beverage of China. Proof of this is that a philosopher of the time, Lu Yu, wrote the first account of its history, cultivation, and preparation in 780 AD: the Cha Ching, or the "Book of Tea."

Tea's reputation reached every corner of China, thanks to caravans of merchants that crisscrossed the country. In 705 AD, *Camellia sinensis* crossed borders for the first time and was introduced in Japan by a monk named Dengyo Daishi. During this same time period, tea arrived in Tibet and was a great success. There they boiled tablets of pressed tea and then mixed it with butter and salt. It wasn't until the start

Tibetan style tea

In his memoir *Seven Years in Tibet*, mountain climber Heinrich Harrer (played in the movie by Brad Pitt) describes the local custom of drinking tea mixed with yak lard, a combination that he found horrifying. The author commented that some Tibetans claimed to drink more than a hundred cups a day.

of the twentieth century that tea in the form of infusion became popular there, although there are still many Tibetans that prefer the traditional preparation.

Beyond China

Tea had begun to cross borders at the beginning of the ninth century, when the first shipments arrived by boat to Korea and Japan. There, a Buddhist monk called Yesai published the first Japanese book on tea in 1191. Both countries began to cultivate tea in the humid, mountainous regions, and their inhabitants soon learned of the therapeutic properties of the infusion. Zen monks incorporated tea in their routines in the temple, in combination with meditation that lasted all day.

Regarding the union between Buddhism and tea, the legend tells that an Indian prince named Drama had decided to devote his life to prayer. Abandoning his home, he began a pilgrimage toward China and Japan. Exhausted from the hard days of journeying, he succumbed to a deep sleep along the banks of a river and slept for a long time. Upon waking, he felt horrified by his laziness and meted himself a severe punishment so as not to succumb to sleep again: he cut off his eyelids and buried them in the place where he had slept. Many years later, returning to his home, he passed that same place and discovered that a strange bush was growing where he had buried the eyelids. The monk chewed a few leaves and realized that they helped keep the mind awake. Since then, the Zen monks always cultivate tea in the monastery gardens.

From "cha" to "tea"

The names given for the word "tea" are very similar throughout Asia: in Japan, it's called *cha*, in Russia *caj*, in India *tschaj* and in China, *ch'a*. Some linguists maintain that it's possible all these names come from the word for "vitality" in Chinese, *chi*.

In the Fukien province of China, the Dutch learned the word *tay*, which means "tea" in the local dialect, and with this sound it was introduced to Europe. In fact, in Ireland and England it was pronounced *tay* until the start of the eighteenth century, after which the word was derived to *tee* and then *tea*—as we know it today.

In many European languages, the same word is used as a generic term for herbal teas or any infusion of herbs.

Apart from making the most of tea's curative properties, the Japanese nobles also began to include tea in their social meetings. Thus was born the *Cha no yu*, the tea ceremony, a delicate and demanding ritual lasting several hours, for which the hosts would have expensive and precious utensils.

Tea arrives in the West

The first record of the existence of tea in the West dates to the year 851 AD. It was written by an Arab merchant named Suleiman in his book *Relations in China and India*, where he defined it as "an aromatic herb with a bitter taste that is drunk with boiled water in the East."

Apparently, westerners did not hear about this infusion again until 1529, when the Venetian Giambattista Ramusio wrote in his book *Navigazione e Viaggi* about the existence about a plant in the East that "calms pain of the gout and also guarantees good stomach function." Jesuit missionaries that visited China and Japan in the sixteenth century also spoke of a plant with a sweet taste that the natives called *chai*.

The East India Company

In the seventeenth century, the European powers competed to claim the new markets in Asia. During this process, the Dutch East India Company brought the first shipment of tea to Europe in 1606. Later, the ships of the English East India Company achieved a monopoly on tea and began to distribute it in France, Germany, and Portugal as well as England. In 1657, the first teahouse opened in London, and financial transactions involving the plant took place on its upper floors. But tea became popular in England a few years later, when King Charles II married Catalina de Berganza, a great fan of the beverage.

The Portuguese princess brought with her dowry the port of Bombay, one of the most important hubs of maritime commerce between Asia and Europe, which became key in the tea trade between the two continents. The infusion began to be served in the court and, during the following century, became the most popular beverage in England, winning over even beer and gin.

In 1834, the East India Company lost its monopoly on tea after the implementation of a British governmental resolution. With free competition between companies, the speed of the ships became more important, so large ships gave way to small, light ships called clippers. This produced true competition to be the first to arrive in port and be able to sell at the best price, resulting in all kinds of incidents and adventures on the high seas, as the typical passage took about a hundred days.

The custom of adding milk to tea—so deeply entrenched in England today—was introduced by the Dutch in the early seventeenth century and then spread to France and England. The Japanese and Chinese never add milk to tea because they believe it ruins the flavor, original color, and aroma of the infusion.

Until the beginning of the nineteenth century, tea was drunk at any time of day. The creation of the British afternoon tea—at five o'clock—is attributed to the Duchess of Bedford, who after drinking it in the afternoon with a snack found it so delicious she instituted the ritual with all her friends.

The spread of tea

In 1810 the Chinese began to cultivate tea on the island of Formosa, in modern-day Taiwan. A decade later in Assam, in the northeastern region of India, Robert Bruce and his brother discovered vast thickets of tea growing naturally and established the tea industry in the then-British colony, including the Darjeeling region.

In other parts of the world tea arrived under more difficult circumstances. In Ceilan, modern-day Sri Lanka, the cultivation of tea began in earnest after a plague affecting coffee trees devastated all the plantations on the island—at that time it was the second-largest producer of coffee in the world.

In each country tea has been introduced differently, with many local variations. The Maghrebis, for example, inherited tea from the English and their national drink is mint tea. It is served in a glass with a lot of sugar, and accompanied by honey cakes. Proper etiquette dictates that the host should drink at least three glasses of tea, with the last one being stronger than the previous.

In 1900, with the inauguration of the Trans-Siberian railroad, tea was no longer transported by camel from Peking to Russia. And four years later, Richard Blechyden presented a refreshing invention at the St. Louis World's Fair: iced tea.

Tea colors

The botanical name for tea is *Camellia sinensis,* which comes from the family Camellia. This is the Chinese variety; in the northeast of India, a second variety known as *Camellia assamica* was discovered in the nineteenth century. The tea bush has leaves with finely serrated edges, with numerous oil glands. The flowers are white and have a delicate fragrance.

The cultivation of tea requires a warm, humid climate, and cultivation at higher altitudes is considered to produce tea of a superior quality, although factors such as the climate, soil, method of harvest, and processing also affect the tea quality.

The majority of teas are made from young leaves. When the bush reaches the necessary maturity, leaves are picked by hand. For the highest quality teas only the top three newest leaves are picked.

After harvesting comes the drying process. The leaves are spread out and left to wilt until they are very malleable and can be rolled without breaking. During this process is when the leaves release the substances that give them their characteristic color and smell.

The giant forest

In 1939, in the province of Yunnan in the southeast of China, a huge swath of wild tea trees were discovered. Some were more than 98 feet (30 meters) high with trunks 3 feet (a meter) in diameter. Their age is estimated to be around 1,700 years old.

Black tea

Green tea

Pu-erh tea

Sencha

Darjeeling badamtan

Genmaicha

Lapsang souchong

Hajua

Russian caravan

Matale

Formosa gunpowder

Jasmine mandarin

Thousand and One Nights

Oolong Sencha

Taj Mahal

Japanese lime

Wild berry

Monk's blend

Rose congou

Earl Grey

Modern and classic teas

The custom of delicately flavored teas has been around for many years; however, fruity teas are a more recent trend and are often closer to an herbal infusion. The ideal choice is always a tea with a truly natural aroma and essence, such as those shown on these pages.

Dream tea

Chai spice tea

Green tea

Green tea is made by drying the leaves completely to avoid fermentation. It is the most common tea consumed in China and Japan. Along with white tea, it has the most proven therapeutic properties.

Green tea tends to have a more delicate and herbal aroma. It has very little theine, or caffeine; depending on the variety, the quantity may be between 8 and 16 mg per cup. By comparison, a cup of espresso can easily have more than 200 mg of caffeine. Here are some of the most highly regarded varieties:

• **Bancha**. Alongside Sencha, although of lesser quality, it is the most common tea in Japan. Very low in theine.

• **Genmaicha**. Green tea with toasted rice; frequently drunk with meals by the Japanese.

• **Gunpowder**. A Chinese tea with a strong flavor, which also appeals to fans of black tea. Often in the form of leaves compressed into a small ball.

• **Kokeicha**. Three-year tea; very valued in Japan. It is made by toasting very fine twigs four times. Then the twigs are pulverized and pressed into fine needles.

• **Kukicha**. Made up of the stems of tea leaves, it makes a yellowish infusion with a distinctive flavor and very little theine.

• **Lung ching**. This tea is the *lung ching* ("dragonwell"). It comes from the lake region of Hangzho, China. It is celebrated for its emerald color and sweet taste.

• **Matcha**. Powdered green tea used in the Japanese tea ceremony; yields a rich, astringent, jade-colored infusion.

• **Sencha**. A Japanese classic. Also available in a decaffeinated version.

Mu Tea. The so-called mu tea does not contain tea leaves; it is actually a unique mixture of sixteen plants and spices, revived in the last few decades from an ancient oriental tradition. It has a very particular taste and is wonderful for digestion. There are truly marvelous stories about its rebalancing powers (see pg. 159).

Black tea

Black tea is obtained through an oxidation process. Freshly harvested leaves are left in humid rooms so they ferment. This treatment lasts between three and five hours depending on the variety, which gives the tea its characteristic dark green or black color.

Black tea has a strong flavor—closer to coffee—and can be combined with milk. It has a higher quantity of caffeine than green tea has. Each cup contains between 25 and 100 mg, depending on the degree of fermentation.

Among the most popular varieties of black tea are:

• **Assam**. A full-bodied tea with a warm brown color. The *Camellia assamica*—a different plant than *Sinensis*—is grown in the northeast region of India.

• **Ceilan**. The ancient name for Sri Lanka is given to this delicate and aromatic black tea. It is commonly sold in bags.

• **Darjeeling**. Called "the champagne of teas" for its delicate fragrance and flavor. It is grown on the slopes of the Indian Himalayas. It is also sold decaffeinated.

• **Earl Grey**. Classic British mix of black tea with bergamot. It is one of the most commonly purchased bagged teas.

Leaves from the sky

The Darjeeling valley is found in the northeast region of India, on the border with Nepal. Eighty-seven tea plantations in this region have a 125-year history. The plant is grown at elevations between 1,970 and 7,050 feet (600 and 2,150 meters), on steep mountainsides that drain heavy monsoon rains.

The tea that grows in this region is of unmatched quality, a bundle of it falling somewhere between sweet grapes and ripe peaches. Between April and May the First Flush is harvested, tender young teas that produce a very light infusion. The second harvest, or Second Flush, occurs in July and August, and produces a bright infusion with a more intense flavor. This is considered ideal for after-dinner drinks.

• **English Breakfast.** Invented by a merchant in the nineteenth century, this is a very strong black tea to help you wake up in the morning.

• **Keemun.** From Chinese, "mountain of the lion." This is a very high-quality tea grown in the humid mountains of Anhui. Its aroma is like that of an orchid.

• **Kenya.** Brightly colored and intensely aromatic, this is one of the black teas with the most body. It is grown at high altitudes in the African country and is usually sold as a powder.

• **Lady Grey.** This is a more fruity—and feminine—version of Earl Grey. In addition to bergamot it contains rose petal and orange peel.

• **Lapsang souchong.** This robust Chinese tea has a characteristic smoky taste, from the process of drying leaves over a wood fire.

• **Samovar.** A very popular mixture developed in Russia from Chinese black tea with a touch of smokiness.

• **Sumatra.** This is a black tea with an intense, but slightly sweet, flavor. It is grown in the Indonesian island of the same name.

Blue tea

This is the name sometimes given to semi-fermented teas, also called Oolong. Instead of completing the oxidation, the fermentation is stopped mid-process—usually after about two hours. The result is a tea halfway between green and black. It has a balanced flavor with a combination of the characteristics of green and black teas, and is very popular in Taiwan. The caffeine content depends on when the fermentation is interrupted and can vary from 10 to 55 mg per cup.

Yellow tea

The leaves of this tea are left to mature rather than ferment. These are varieties that are difficult to find commercially. The yellow tea takes its name from the color of the infusion it produces. It has a singular and defined taste that can be slightly bitter. Its fresh scent leaves the mouth clean and dry. Its flavor—somewhere between sweet and bitter—lingers on the tip of the tongue after drinking it.

Chun Shan Yin Chin is considered the best and most valuable yellow tea. Mao-chien and Huang Da Cha are other popular varieties.

Red tea

There is some confusion about what is popularly known as "red tea." The Chinese give this name to *Pu-erh*, a variety of green tea that only grows in the Yunnan region and is fermented to darken it. This "tea of the Emperor," so called because it originally was reserved only for the highest offices of power, is frequently used in diets today because of its "fat-eliminating" qualities.

Sometimes "red tea" is used to refer to Rooibos, a South African plant with a sweet taste and invigorating and healing properties, which belongs to a botanical family unrelated to tea.

More information on Pu-erh tea and Rooibos can be found in the bibliography on pg. 165.

White tea

White tea is grown in many parts of China. It is lightly fermented and gives a very lightly colored infusion. In some plants, the leaf appears to have a white fuzz. The buds are harvested just two days of the year, in spring, and are picked by hand. It takes approximately 80,000 buds to produce only 250 grams of tea; this is why the price is so high.

The legend of the white tea

Popular tradition tells that in ancient China, this type of tea was harvested exclusively by maidens with gold scissors, and that only the emperor had the right to taste it. The location of the sacred gardens was itself a mystery, and those few who discovered it paid with their lives. *Pai Hao Yin Chin* is a fairytale about this white tea.

In Fujian there was once a drought so severe that nothing could be harvested for many seasons. Then a plague ravaged the country and many people died. The situation got worse and worse and the elders recommended they go search for a sacred plant that grew beside the well of a dragon, in a nearby mountain. The juice of this plant, they said, would bring back the land's prosperity and cure the sick.

Many brave young people from Fujian went to the mountains in search of this sacred plant, but none of them returned, since the well was guarded by a fierce black dragon. Two brothers and their sister decided to go on the search. The oldest was the first to go, but he did not return. The second departed and suffered the same fate. Finally, the younger sister decided to go in search of her brothers and the plant. When she got there, she found that the dragon had turned the men to stone. Using her wits, she managed to steal the plant and kill the dragon with an arrow. With a few drops of the sacred plants, she brought the men back to life and they returned to the town and planted the seeds. The land became fertile once more and the sick were healed.

From that day on, all of the plants in Fujian, a province at an altitude of 6000 meters, were of white tea, which is grown there to this day.

White tea has a much softer taste and scent than the other teas, and it contains the least amount of theine: about 1 mg per cup. It is highly valued for its therapeutic properties, since its antioxidant power is triple that of green tea. The most well-known varieties are Shou mei, Pai hao Yin chin, and Pai mu tan.

Aromatic teas

Normally these are made from lower-quality leaves. In western shops, they are most often mixes based on black tea, although there are some classics made with green tea like that of jasmine—highly valued in China—or that of Japanese lime.

Tea gourmets always prefer the pure varieties, but if they are to consume an aromatic tea, they opt for flower accents.

The fragrance of the flowers is incorporated into the leaves during processing.

It is essential to achieve the right balance between tea and the flowers so the fragrance does not cover the natural flavor of the tea. According to experts, the flower should make up about 30 percent of the taste and the tea should be the other 70 percent. In and of itself, the type of flower depends on the type of tea. Teas with a stronger flavor allow for the incorporation of more concentrated fragrances.

The flowers most commonly used are jasmine, rose, lychee, and lotus.

Therapeutic properties

No one doubts the numerous health benefits of tea, especially green tea, or its direct relation to the high longevity index in some parts of China and Japan.

In addition to its gentle stimulating action, regular tea consumption has a very positive effect on the body. The following ten points summarize the fabulous properties of this natural ally to beauty and health.

1. Stops ageing
Free radicals attack cells, oxidizing their membranes, which in turn damages DNA and causes ageing in general. The polyphenols and catechins in green tea have an antioxidant action twenty times that of vitamin E.

2. Protects against cancer
Numerous studies show that the consumption of green tea in Japan—5 or 6 cups a day on average—is closely linked to the low rates of cancer compared to Western countries. It is believed that the tannins and catechins protect cells from the processes that deteriorate them.

3. Keeps cholesterol at bay
High levels of cholesterol are associated with many illnesses, the most prominent among them being heart disease. The catechins in green tea control … the excess of

Cholesterol

The level of cholesterol in our body is measured in milligrams per deciliter of blood. If the HDL, or "good cholesterol," is low and the LDL, or "bad cholesterol," is too high, the risk of heart disease increases. Your cholesterol levels can be detected through a blood test.

Risk index	HDL	LDL
Low	more than 65	lower than 130
Medium	35–64	130–159
High	34 or lower	160 or higher

"bad cholesterol" in the blood. Tea is, as we will see, a great ally to our circulatory system.

4. Combats hypertension

Experiments performed in labs have shown that daily tea consumption prevents arterial hypertension. The natural catechins in green tea and its high vitamin E content have a lot to do with this.

5. Prevents cardiovascular disease

Tea is an important source of vitamin E, an essential element to prevent cardiovascular disease, since it helps dissolve blood clots, prevents plaque buildups, and helps phagocytes do their job.

6. Stimulates the body's defenses

Green tea is a great reinforcement for the immune system, thanks to Epigallocatechin gallate (EGCG), which stimulates the production of lymphocytes B and T—tiny cells that make up the backbone of the immune system. The polyphenols in green tea help both types of lymphocytes reproduce, increasing the body's immune response.

Less fermentation, more catechins

The proportion of catechins in different types of tea depends on the processing they have been subjected to. Green tea, which doesn't undergo any fermentation process, can contain up to 30 percent of catechins, which means it has a greater curative power than other types of tea with a lower proportion. Oolong, which is semi-fermented, can have a maximum of 20 percent of catechins while black tea, which is more fermented, contains less than 10 percent of its total weight in catechins.

7. Protects against the flu

The catechins and teoflavins can act strongly against the flu virus, so tea is especially recommended for the elderly. Some studies suggest that it even has an effect against the diseases associated with HIV.

8. Invigorates the body and mind

Tea is a gentle stimulant, much less offensive than coffee. It renews energy in the whole body, fights off tiredness, and boosts intellectual capabilities.

9. Relieves skin conditions

Bathing in green tea or applying it with a hot compress can be an effective treatment for athlete's foot or numerous other skin afflictions.

10. Prevents cavities

Black tea contains teoflavins that help stop the activity of a bacterium called *streptococcus mutans*, which causes cavities. The catechins in green tea do this as well, but also prevent the bacteria from adhering to teeth. Thus, green tea has the most powerful antibacterial action, followed by Pu-erh, black tea, and lastly, Oolong.

The ten benefits of Pu-erh tea

Traditional Chinese Medicine considers this red tea to be a prime remedy to promote good health and weight loss. In addition to being a fat burner, it has so many therapeutic virtues that it was once known as "the tea of the emperors." Some of these properties are:

1. Detoxes and purifies
2. Strengthens the immune system
3. Reduces bad moods and even mild depression
4. Stimulates the secretion of digestive juices
5. Eases the digestion of fatty foods
6. Reduces the level of fat in the blood
7. Eliminates excess weight caused by poor nutrition
8. Lowers cholesterol levels
9. Stimulates liver function and metabolism
10. Protects the body from infections through its antibacterial properties.

Tea versus coffee

Although tea and coffee both contain caffeine, there are important differences in the way that both beverages affect the body. First off, no study has been able to prove that coffee provides notable health benefits, and it can even be the source of some disorders. Without going too much into it, coffee increases the proportion of fatty acids in the blood, while tea, especially green tea, has anti-arteriosclerotic effects.

The caffeine in coffee is absorbed much more quickly than that in tea—also called theine—although the effect of the latter is more prolonged.

Coffee can easily provoke insomnia, since it stimulates the heart and accelerates the circulation of blood. Tea can also provoke insomnia—given that theine affects the central nervous system—but the effect is very different depending on whether it is black tea or green tea.

The stimulant action of green tea is much gentler than that of black tea, which is in turn harsher on the stomach. Either way, black tea is more digestible than coffee, and green tea in particular is an alkaline beverage that counteracts the acidity of the stomach.

Other plants that contain caffeine

There are many other plants in the world, in addition to tea and coffee, that contain caffeine. Cacao seeds contain between 0.05 and 0.4 percent caffeine. Kola nuts contain between 1.5 and 3.5 percent. Another plant with natural caffeine content is *maté*, which originates in subtropical South America, and contains between 0.3 and 1.5 percent in its leaves.

Lastly, there is guarana, the seeds of which contain between 4 and 8 percent caffeine and are used to make energy drinks.

Caffeine under control

According to some doctors, daily caffeine intake should not exceed 200 mg. The following table shows the milligrams of caffeine per cup or glass.

Drink	
Coffee (from a coffee maker)	115
Instant coffee	80
Decaf coffee	3
Green tea	15
Black tea	40
Mate	31
Cocoa	4
Colas	20

How to control theine

It's possible to regulate the amount of theine as you prepare tea. Depending on the steeping time, you can determine how stimulating the tea will be.

Since theine or caffeine is a substance that dissolves in hot water, if you let the infusion steep for one or two minutes, it will concentrate quickly. This results in a high content of theine, which passes through the body rapidly.

Alternately, if you leave the infusion to steep longer, between four and ten minutes, the tea will be stronger but the theine will have less of an effect on the body. This is because the tannins, which slow down the absorption of theine, have more time to dissolve and are present in higher concentrations.

Tea and sports

Because of its energizing and revitalizing properties, green tea is the perfect drink for before, during, and after exercise. Its gentle stimulant action—which doesn't reach the point of causing nervousness—promotes mental agility, concentration, motivation, and resistance, even for activities lasting hours.

Strictly on the physical plane, tea increases the body's vital energy thanks to its combination of active ingredients, with a high proportion of vitamin C and other vitamins.

As an isotonic drink, with a few drops of lemon, it is very effective at quenching the thirst that comes from physical activity. In order to balance the levels of blood sugar during exercise, you can sweeten it with honey or maple syrup.

Green tea during menopause and pregnancy

Many women experience hormonal changes during menopause that often cause mood swings and restlessness.

During gestation, women usually take vitamin and mineral supplements, with a special focus on iron. On top of a healthy diet, many specialists recommend that women switch from coffee to green tea during pregnancy. If we compare the two beverages, we find that coffee reduces or even blocks the absorption of iron and other minerals, while green tea provides an important dose of iron and zinc.

Tea also promotes energy and optimism. However, it's important to remember that pregnant women are often more sensitive to caffeine. Therefore, in order to avoid problems with insomnia, note the following advice before drinking tea in the afternoon or at night.

- Green tea is preferable because it has a lower theine content than fermented teas.
- Bancha tea is another healthy option because it contains all the active ingredients that are important for health, with much less caffeine.
- A trick for reducing theine: pour a little boiling water over dry tea leaves and strain after thirty seconds. Then make the tea as usual.

Precautions for tea drinkers

1. Children under the age of two should not drink tea, since it interferes with iron absorption and can cause anemia.

2. Don't drink very concentrated tea unless it's for specific medicinal purposes.

3. Wait a few minutes before drinking a fresh infusion. It is easy to burn yourself with hot tea.

4. Cold tea can impede digestion.

5. Do not drink reheated tea from the day before.

6. To enjoy all its benefits, tea should be made from good quality water.

7. Do not drink tea after eating lamb, as it hardens the stomach and causes constipation.

8. If you suffer from stomach ulcers, it's best not to drink tea, as it can interfere with the absorption of nutrients.

9. Excess tea consumption can stress the kidneys because of its diuretic effect.

10. If you have a delicate stomach, tea on an empty stomach can provoke nausea, vomiting, and stomach pains.

11. Tea contracts the muscles of the stomach. If you drink too much before a meal it can ruin your appetite.

12. It's inadvisable to drink tea less than an hour before or after taking medication.

13. Women who take birth control pills shouldn't drink very strong tea.

14. During menstruation, tea can increase blood flow.

15. People with hypertension shouldn't drink tea that is too concentrated, as it can raise blood pressure.

Low vitality leads many women to drink more coffee, which reduces the absorption of many elements necessary for the body—such as calcium and iron—and doesn't improve their emotional state at all.

Green tea contains active ingredients that can be vital during this period. Recent studies have shown that some substances found in tea complement, or are even better than, vitamin E and can help slow the ageing process. Its effect is also emotionally very beneficial.

Because of all this, specialists consider green tea to be a tremendous help to health and well-being during the menopause years.

Green tea and diets

Every year dozens of new diets come out claiming to help you slim down. However, in most of them the harm it does the body is greater than the hypothetical benefits.

The majority of diets are based on insufficient or unbalanced nutrition, since they are designed with just one goal in mind, either weight loss or being beneficial to a specific organ.

This is why, when one decides to fast it's best to switch to green tea and give up black tea or coffee.

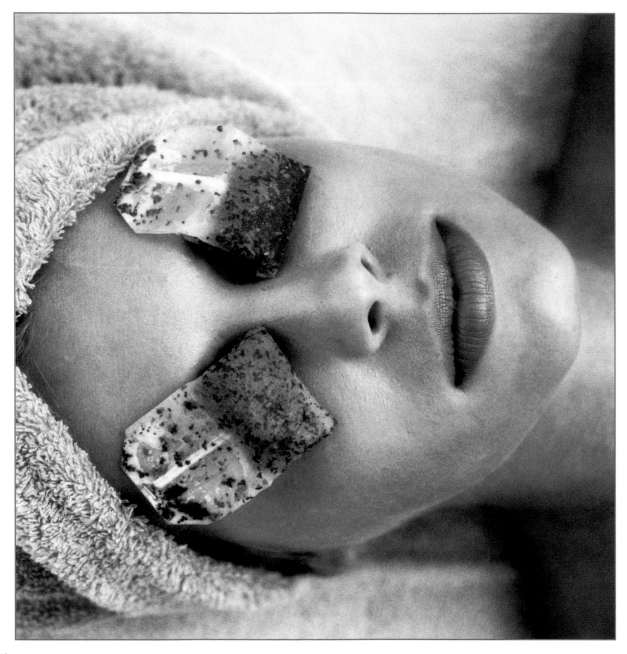

Other household uses

Although tea is known mainly as a beverage, it's a plant with extraordinary properties that can have many other uses. Let's see twelve interesting uses for *Camellia sinensis*.

Tea bath

For a revitalizing and purifying bath, put a handful of green tea leaves, already boiled, into a mesh bag, secure shut, and submerge it in the hot bath water. You can also use used tea bags.

Eye relief

To calm and refresh tired eyes, you can apply a used tea bag (wet and lukewarm) to cover each eyelid for five to ten minutes.

Mouthwash

Gargling with green tea can help fight bad breath and kill bacteria in the mouth. The natural fluoride in tea also contributes to strengthen tooth enamel and prevent diseases such as gingivitis. You don't have to use a first infusion for this; you can drink the first two and then boil the leaves for the third time for the mouthwash.

Tea bags

In the East they use old green tea leaves—called *chagara*—to make decorative, aromatic bags. To maintain them, it's best to air them out once a week. The subtle aroma of tea is great for relaxation and to help you sleep.

Incense

Whether in a bar, cone, or as an essential oil, green tea has a delicate, pleasant aroma that promotes harmony and concentration. This should not be confused with "tea tree" oil, which has other uses, such as disinfecting.

Preparing fish or meat

If you wash fish with tea before frying, it will reduce the strong fishy odor and eliminate bacteria. This is why the Japanese drink tea with sushi or sashimi—raw fish. Cooking pork in tea—including the leaves—reduces the level of fat and cholesterol in the meat.

Air freshener for the refrigerator

A bag of dry green tea leaves—*chagara*—helps eliminate bad odors in the refrigerator. However, you should not keep tea for your consumption in the fridge, as the smells of other foods can overpower the tea's delicate flavor.

Cleaning cutting boards

A common problem with wood cutting boards is it's difficult to eliminate the odor, especially from fish or meat, even after cleaning with soap and water.

Green tea is very useful in this case: rub wet chagara over the surface of the used wood, leaving a layer for a few minutes. Then remove the leaves and rinse with water. Tea liqueur also works to clean cutting boards and other utensils.

Natural beauty with green tea

Lately green tea is used a lot in beauty products to fight the marks of ageing and damage from UV rays, either as a principal ingredient or combined with other natural products. In many cosmetic stores you can find the following products made with green tea:

— Facial cleansers
— Moisturizing lotions and creams
— Sunscreen
— Toners and body masks
— Shampoos, dyes, and other hair care products
— Perfumes

For those who love home remedies, washing your face with green tea helps clean impurities and blackheads. It's also good for hair: adding it to the last rinse will make hair soft and shiny.

Preventing rust

A secret among eastern cooks: rubbing the pots and pans with chagara prevents rust on kitchen utensils, as the tannins from the tea form a thin protective film on the surface of the steel.

Cleaning rugs

Since tea has the ability to absorb unpleasant odors, we can use chagara to deodorize and eliminate bacteria from carpets and rugs. Before vacuuming, dust the surface with dry green tea leaves and let sit for a few minutes. All you have to do after is vacuum, which will pick up the dust and the tea leaves. Along with cleaning the rug, it will also leave a nice fresh scent in the room.

Mosquito repellant

Good news for those who suffer plagues of mosquito bites every summer: burnt tea leaves repel mosquitoes. You can put some dry tea leaves in an incense burner and light them so that they smoke for a few minutes.

Plant fertilizer

Used tea is an excellent fertilizer for all kinds of plants, since it has valuable organic nutrients. If you use bags, you can even bury them whole in the pots.

Tea in the home

Secrets of preparation

In ancestral Japan, masters of tea reached such a spiritual connection with the preparation of tea that they practically flowed with every movement. Contradictory to the complex protocol of the tea ceremony—which we will see in the next chapter—Rikyu, one of the most celebrated masters, said:

> *Tea is nothing more than this:*
> *You boil the water*
> *You fill it with tea*
> *And you drink it…*
> *That's all there is to know.*

In this chapter, we'll look at how to complete this simple process to enjoy a heavenly cup of tea.

Storing

Fresh tea leaves are a prerequisite for making a quality infusion. Tea easily picks up the odor of other foods, and its own aroma can be fragile. For maximum freshness, it should be stored in airtight containers of metal or porcelain. Glass is not recommended, since light and moisture can alter the properties of tea.

The teapot

Experts insist that you should never wash the inside of the teapot. At most, you can rinse it and let it dry. The reason is that soap breaks down the fine film that forms on the interior of the pot—one of the secrets of a good tea shop—and can leave chemical residues that contaminate the flavor.

It's important that the teapot itself is used exclusively to serve tea. Gourmets recommend having three different teapots: one for classic teas, one for smoked teas, and another for aromatic teas.

The cups

To appreciate the color of the infusion, it's best to choose white or pale cream porcelain cups, or transparent glasses like those used in Arabic countries for mint tea.

The water

The other key is the water used to make the tea. It is best to use only mineral water so that the leaves can reveal all their nuances.

The first secret of tea

—"Is this the first time you've been to the land of tea, Mr. Stowe?"

—"It's actually the first time I've visited China."

—"Then I should tell you the first of the three secrets of tea," said Wang. He clapped and immediately a servant appeared with a silver tray with three steaming cups of tea.

Charles Stowe took one and lifted it to his lips. The infusion was delicious.

—"Is this the tea you produce here?" he asked.

—". . . And better teas exist as well. But the water that was used to make this one is the purest of all the empire."

He stood and went to the jade fountain. He filled a glass with water and held it out for Charles Stowe. He drank it in a gulp. It was the purest water he had ever tasted. The Englishman looked at the fountain and asked:

—"Where does this water come from?"

—"From a spring in the mountain. That is the first secret: if the water is not excellent, neither is the tea."

Maxence Fermine, *Opium*

The three infusions

Green tea leaves can be used up to three times. In fact, some experts insist that the second cup is the best. They believe that the first cup is too strong and the third is too thin.

After the second infusion, the leaves—already tender—should steep for only half the usual time. In any case, the second and third infusions should be made the same day, since too much time can alter the natural properties of the tea leaves.

Five golden rules

1. **Heat the teapot.** It's enough to just fill it with hot water before adding the tea. In winter you can also heat the cups. This is essential, since this heats the leaves, allowing them to release their aroma.

2. **Put one level teaspoon of tea per cup, plus one for the teapot.** Cover the teapot immediately and let it rest for three minutes in the pot. There are many types of filters—of porcelain, clay, or metal—for this purpose, but the best is cloth. Experts advise against the perforated balls that you submerge in the teapot or cup, since they press the tea and don't allow the leaves to expand during steeping.

3. **Pour the water before it boils.** Or, if it has already boiled, wait until all the bubbles disappear before filling the teapot. In fact, purists say that you should never use water that has already reached boiling point. There are even electric kettles that stop automatically at 203°F (95°C).

4. **Let steep for two to five minutes.** Five minutes is the maximum time that the leaves can be in contact with the water, if you want a more bitter or astringent infusion, with lower theine content that has a longer effect. If you steep for only two minutes, on the other hand, you will have a more stimulating infusion, with a light aromatic flavor.

5. **Fill the cups in two turns.** After throwing out the hot water—if you've preheated the cups—pour a little bit of tea in each cup and then pour a second round, filling each teacup to the top. This way each cup will have the same taste and quality.

Tricks to eliminate theine

It's estimated that approximately 80 percent of theine—or caffeine—is released in the first 30 seconds of the infusion.

Therefore, people who are especially sensitive, or want to drink tea in the afternoon without staying up late, can follow this simple process.

1. Pour boiling water over the tea leaves.
2. Let the leaves steep for 30 seconds.
3. Remove the water, leaving the pre-soaked leaves.
4. Prepare the tea as usual.

Iced tea

For iced tea, people typically use black tea flavored with peach or lemon, although there are countless other recipes to suit all tastes. It is very easy to make: make an infusion twice as strong as usual and let refrigerate for twelve hours.

Iced tea is usually sweetened, so you can add brown sugar or maple syrup.

Tea ceremony

A thousand years ago

The origin of the Japanese tea ceremony can be found approximately a thousand years ago, when the Japanese nobles incorporated the beverage into their daily rituals. They competed among themselves to have the most beautiful, finely made instruments, which indicated the social status of the family, and elaborated a long, complex ceremony called Cha no yu, or "Way of the tea."

The ritual, whose spirit has survived to this day, began with a silent welcome as the host toasted his guests from the garden gate.

Many nobles had a tea house apart from the home especially for this ceremony, decorated with a centerpiece of simple flowers in a decorative basket.

Once everyone was gathered, the host lit the fire and offered each guest a light meal of soup, legumes, and sweets. Once the meal was finished, the plates were removed and the guests washed their mouths and hands.

Next, the host would put three spoonfuls of powdered green tea in a bowl and add a little bit of hot water.

When the dough was well thickened, the host offered the bowl to the guest of honor, who rested the bowl in the palm of his left hand and held it with the fingers of his right hand.

After the first sip, it was customary for the host to ask the guest of honor his opinion of the tea served, and the guest would inquire about the origin and variety of the plant. Then, the guest of honor passed the bowl to the rest of the guests.

Once all the guests had tried the tea, which happened in total silence, the ceremony was over.

Here and now

This beautiful ritual persists a little differently to this day in Japan and it has a very strict code of conduct. The conversation during the ceremony, for example, should never be about politics or any other subject that could cause conflict or make the guests uncomfortable. The host and the guests should avoid bragging or praising any of the present guests.

The tea houses are decorated very simply, prioritizing elegance of the form over irrelevant details. The silence, the harmony of the colors… the general atmosphere is essential for the purpose of this ritual, which is to reclaim calm at the end of a busy day.

The French orientalist and yoga teacher Henri Brunel captures the spirit of the Cha no yu with great mastery in his books. First off though, let's review the necessary ingredients for a tea ceremony:

- A modest and tranquil place
- Embrace the moment
- Pleasant and calm behavior between friends
- Care and love in the preparation of the "golden elixir": the tea
- Contemplation of simple and beautiful objects
- Silence

Kaiseki

The tea ceremony traditionally took half a day to complete all the phases: the meal, a thick infusion, and afterward a more diluted infusion. Between these "three dishes,"

the guests usually relaxed in the garden or in a space designed for this purpose. The pauses were an opportunity for the host to switch out some of the artworks in the room, so that the guests could contemplate them when the ritual continued.

Likewise he/she would rearrange the flowers and stoke the fire, a process that recalls the maxim: "Change everything so nothing changes."

The term *kaiseki*—the meal served during the tea ceremony—originally referred to the flat stones, heated over the fire, that Zen monks laid over their stomachs to calm their hunger during long hours of meditation. Now it refers to the small delicacies offered to guests after the infusion.

A typical *kaiseki* consists of rice, broth with lemon, grilled fish with ginger, seaweed salad with steamed roe, and mushrooms. This meal is usually accompanied by sake, Japanese rice wine. Curiously, the host never drinks or eats with his guests during the kaiseki, since he/she must be attentive to the conversation and make sure it follows the ceremonial norms.

The rotation of the bowl

An important aspect of the tea ceremony is the way you hold the bowl in which they serve the tea. The Japanese don't drink tea from a cup with a handle, like westerners, but rather in small bowls decorated with a natural motif. This may evoke the branch of a tree, leaves, or maybe a flower, and serves to distinguish the front part of the bowl from the back.

The decorated—or more colorful—face should always be facing the host as he/she prepares the tea, then turned toward the guest in the moment the tea is served. When the guests taste the tea, the front of the bowl should once again face toward the host.

The bowl is always held in the right hand, the same hand that rotates the bowl through the course of the ceremony. The left hand only supports the bowl.

"Let us imagine a remote path, in a mountain or a forest, that leads to the dwelling of a wise man. There we see the tea pavilion appear. Its construction is simple, of wood and bamboo. Here the aim is not to oppose time, or idolize it with a ridiculous eternity of stone, but to "embrace" it.

The room into which we enter is modest on the surface: about nine square meters (two and a half rush mats); three or four friends fit comfortably. A Zen painting, a bouquet of wildflowers are the only adornment. The hearth of coal, of wood, the round iron boiler covered in patina, the water jug, the bamboo ladle, an immaculate white cloth, the jars of tea, the traditional bowls.

The tea master completes the ritual gestures skillfully, slowly, carefully, and lovingly. The conversation goes by, pleasantly; we talk of poetry, of history, of architecture. Very gently, the soft sounds of voices grow quiet, and we all contemplate in silence the family bowls, a wildflower; in the distance, we hear birdsong.

Time is suspended, in harmony, serenity."

Henri Brunel, *The most beautiful stories of Zen*, Ed. J.J. Olañeta

Hot or cold sake?

This traditional Japanese rice liquor can be served cold, at room temperature, or heated by bathing the jar in warm water. In most restaurants, if the sake is of high quality, it is served lightly chilled, as specialists say that only cheap sake should be warmed. However, sake was originally served hot, including during the tea ceremony. Many *sakaguras*—sake distilleries—label each type with the best way to drink it.

Once the tea has been enjoyed, the bowl is set on the table and the guest pauses for a few seconds, contemplating with their eyes on the bottom of the bowl.

The tea ritual in China

In China, tea is such a common element that even the word for "restaurant" in the language means "house of tea."

According to ancient custom, many people slurped tea noisily with the help of a spoon. This permitted them to perceive all the complexity and nuances of the flavor, but today hardly anyone does it because it's considered poor manners.

The contemporary Chinese drink ch'a in small sips from a handleless cup. Some of them eat the tea leaves that are left in the bottom of the cup.

In either case, in China they don't drink tea just to quench thirst or wake up. It is a social act that allows people to chat, gossip, or talk business. Tea is also present in many rituals. When someone receives a guest in their home, for example, it is essential to serve a cup as a welcoming gesture. The rituals of tea became a vital means of communication and socialization in China. One of them was the proposal, originally practiced in the countryside and then popularized in the city. When a young man was interested in a young woman, he sent a messenger to her parents' house with tea leaves as a gift.

The family then prepared the tea and, if they drank it, it meant that they gave their blessing for the marriage. If, on the other hand, they left it intact, it meant they rejected the suitor.

Similarly, to ask forgiveness of an older person, one would offer them tea, and the means of giving a response was the same.

Even today, when a young person asks a teacher of arts or martial arts to accept them as a student, they follow the same ritual. If the teacher drinks the tea, it means they accept the student.

During the Chinese Revolution, the different revolutionary groups distinguished themselves by their manner of drinking tea, employing a complex code of hand signals as they prepared the cups and teapot and poured and drank the tea.

The majority of Chinese homes, both in the country and abroad, have a small altar. Each day, the family leaves a gift of tea, fruit, and incense, in honor of their ancestors, the gods, and the spirits.

Tea ceremony

Drinks and culinary recipes

Quantities:
Unless otherwise indicated,
the recipes are for 3–4 servings
and the amount of water is 800 ml.

Infusions and tisanes
Iced green tea with cinnamon

Ingredients:

5 or 6 teaspoons green tea

½ cinnamon stick

1 tablespoon honey

1 teaspoon lemon juice

Angostura bitters

1. In a saucepan, combine water, the tea, and the cinnamon stick chopped into pieces.

2. Let boil, then strain.

3. Add honey, lemon juice, and a few drops of angostura while the infusion is still hot.

4. Leave in the fridge to cool.

COLD, BUT NOT FROZEN

Iced tea keeps well in the fridge, but before serving it's best to leave it for a few minutes at room temperature. Drinks that are too cold can negatively affect the kidneys and bladder.

While you wait for it to "thaw" a little, you can garnish the tea with a mint leaf or slice of lemon or orange.

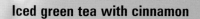

Iced green tea with cinnamon

thee
tea
thé
te
chay
tee
teja
cha
ta
tey
ch'a

Lemon balm tea with passion flower, poppy, and orange blossom

Isotonic tea

Ingredients:
5 or 6 teaspoons green tea
1 or 2 teaspoons honey
a few drops lemon juice

1. Heat water in a pot and remove from heat just before it boils.
2. Pour water over the tea and, while still hot, add the honey and lemon juice.
3. Strain into a thermos if you want to keep it hot, or a water bottle if you want to let it cool.

Lemon balm tea with passion flower, poppy, and orange blossom

Helps you fall asleep and rest well.

Ingredients:
1 oz (30 g) lemon balm leaves
1 oz (30 g) passion flower
0.7 oz (20 g) poppy petals
0.7 oz (20 g) orange blossom

1. Combine all ingredients in a saucepan and cover with water. Bring to a boil for 30 seconds, then turn off the heat. Cover and let rest for 10 minutes.
2. Strain the infusion and sweeten with honey to taste. Drink in small sips after dinner. *(More therapeutic teas and tisanes on pg. 108).*

Infusions and tisanes

Green tea with mint

Green tea with mint

Ingredients:
2 handfuls fresh mint
2½ cups (600 ml) infusion green tea
1 tablespoon honey
1 tablespoon lemon juice

1. In a saucepan, mix one cup of green tea, the honey, and the mint.
2. When it begins to boil, leave on low heat for 10 minutes.
3. Let cool, strain, and add the lemon juice and remaining green tea.
4. Serve with ice, garnished with a slice of lemon and a sprig of mint.

Party tea

Ingredients:
4¼ cups (1 l) infusion green tea
0.9 oz (25 g) mint leaves
1 cup (250 ml) orange juice
1 cup (250 ml) lemon juice
21 oz (600 g) orange honey
Ice cubes
Lemon and orange wedges

1. Add the honey to a saucepan with 1 cup of water. Over medium heat, stir the mixture until it reaches a boil and the honey has dissolved.
2. Add the mint leaves and cook over low heat for 5 minutes.
3. When the mixture is cooled, combine with the rest of the ingredients in a punch bowl.
4. Serve with ice and garnish with the fruit wedges.

Gentian, thyme, elderberry, and poppy tea

Tea cocktail

Ingredients:
1¼ cups (300 ml) green tea infusion
7 oz (200 g) honey
1 cup (250 ml) orange juice
7 oz (200 g) diced fresh fruit
2 cans ginger ale
crushed ice

1. Mix all ingredients except the ginger ale and ice, which should be added just before serving.
2. If the cocktail is too strong, you can dilute it with water or a little more ginger ale.

Gentian, thyme, elderberry, and poppy tea
An excellent cold remedy

Ingredients:
1.4 oz (40 g) sliced gentian root
1.25 oz (35 g) thyme flowers and leaves
0.5 oz (15 g) elderberry flower
0.35 oz (10 g) poppy petals

1. Mix the ingredients and use 1 tablespoon of the mixture per tea cup.
2. Boil for 2 minutes, cover, and let rest for 20 minutes, strain.

Drink in small sips two or three times a day. This tea provides relief from cold and flu symptoms. Not recommended for pregnant or lactating women.

A candle in a small glass
helps keep tea warm

"Chai high" tea

Ingredients:
3 slices ginger
6 cloves
½ teaspoon coriander seeds
1 cinnamon stick
¼ teaspoon anise seeds
2½ tablespoons black tea leaves
3 cups (750 ml) hot water
1 cup (250 ml) milk
2 tablespoons honey

1. Heat all the dry ingredients in a covered frying pan over very low heat for 5 to 10 minutes, without letting them toast.

2. Bring the water to a boil, and then combine with the dry ingredients.

3. After a couple of minutes, strain the chai tea into a teapot. Cover the teapot with a towel or teapot cover to keep the chai hot.

Described as a "sensual nectar," this tea stimulates friendly conversation after a good dinner. In North America it's also called "Saturday night tea."

A CANDLE TO KEEP THE TEA WARM

In specialty shops you can find a teapot stand designed to hold a small candle, which is meant to keep the infusion hot for several hours. It's best not to use scented candles, since the strong essences in the candle can ruin the delicate aroma of the tea.

Lemon green tea

Ingredients:
1 cup (250 ml) lemonade
3 cups (750 ml) green tea infusion
brown sugar and lemon juice

1. Mix the lemonade with the infusion and store in the refrigerator.
2. Take the glasses, wet the rims with lemon juice, and dip in the brown sugar to coat them. Leave the prepared glasses in the freezer for at least 10 minutes before pouring the tea.
3. Garnish the glasses with mint leaves and pour the tea carefully so as not to ruin the sugar coating.

Spiced green tea

Ingredients:
4 teaspoons green tea
orange and lemon peels
grated nutmeg and whole vanilla bean
0.7 oz (20 g) cane sugar
3 cups (750 ml) orange juice
lemon juice

1. Put the tea in a teapot and add the orange and lemon peels, a little nutmeg, and the vanilla bean.
2. Add the cane sugar and pour boiling water over the mixture. Cover to let steep and cool.
3. Add orange juice, a few drops of lemon juice, and crushed ice (if desired) just before serving. ♪

Spiced green tea

Apple tea

Ingredients:
4 bags green tea
4¼ cups (1 l) apple juice
6 cinnamon sticks
6 vanilla beans
orange or lemon peel, cut in strips

1. Bring the apple juice to a boil.
2. Put the tea bags in the teapot and prepare the infusion for 2 or 3 minutes.
3. Decorate the glasses with strips of orange or lemon peel.
4. Add 1 stick of cinnamon and 1 vanilla bean to 6 glasses and cover with the hot tea.

Vanilla, cinnamon, and clove spiced tea

Ingredients:
3.5 oz (100 g) low-theine green tea
4¼ cups (1 l) water
2 or 3 vanilla beans
3 or 4 cinnamon sticks
2 cloves
a few drops Angostura bitters
honey to taste

1. Grind the cinnamon, vanilla, and cloves with a mortar and pestle.
2. Combine the paste with the green tea leaves.
3. Put 5 or 6 teaspoons of the mixture into the water and bring to a boil.
4. Strain, then finish with a few drops of Angostura and honey.

Spiced winter tea

Ingredients:
6 bags green tea
1 cup (250 ml) orange juice
1 cup (250 ml) pineapple juice
1 tablespoon allspice
1 teaspoon clove
2 cinnamon sticks
2 vanilla beans
0.7 oz (20 g) cane sugar
2 teaspoons honey
orange slices

1. Prepare an infusion with the tea bags, steep for 5 minutes, and remove the bags. Then add all the ingredients except the cinnamon and orange slices.
2. Bring to a boil and let simmer for 2 or 3 minutes.
3. Stir with the cinnamon sticks so that the tea takes on the flavor only very lightly.
4. Serve hot and garnish with orange slices.

YOGI TEA

The last two recipes may sound a bit like the famous "yogi tea" based on the spices they contain. However, authentic yogi tea that is made and drank in ayurvedic centers in India doesn't usually contain actual tea. The classic ingredients of this energetic brew—often drunk with milk—are cinnamon, cardamom, ginger, cloves, and black pepper.

Flaming tea

Ingredients:

2 cups (½ l) strong black tea
1 large glass black rum
3 strips of orange peel
½ lemon
½ vanilla bean, chopped
1 clove
1 pinch cinnamon
cane sugar or honey

1. In a bowl, combine two tablespoons of rum, along with the vanilla bean, clove, cinnamon, and orange peel.
2. Let marinate for about an hour, then strain.
3. Bring the black tea to a boil then and combine with the strained rum infusion. Season with lemon juice and sweeten to taste.
4. Pour the tea into a punch bowl and add the rest of the rum, and ignite.
5. Serve immediately.

Iced tea with sherry

Ingredients:

4¼ cups (1 l) black tea
1 glass sherry
1 lemon, sliced
cane sugar

1. Prepare the infusion, add sugar to taste, and chill.
2. Add the sherry and refrigerate a few hours.
3. Serve in a glass with a slice of lemon.

Tea slushie

Ingredients:

4¼ cups (1 l) infusion of a tea of your choice
cane sugar
mint leaves

    1. Prepare the infusion, add sugar to taste, and let chill.
    2. Freeze in ice cube trays.
    3. Crush in a blender and serve with mint leaves as garnish.

Tea sangria

Ingredients:

4¼ cups (1 l) infusion strong black tea
1 grapefruit
½ pineapple
2 peaches in syrup
juice of one lemon
cane sugar

    1. Prepare the infusion and sweeten to taste.
    2. Slice the fruit and add to the tea in a jar.
    3. Finish with the lemon juice, mix well, and chill several hours in the fridge.
    4. Serve with ice.

Tea milkshake

Ingredients:

4¼ cups (1 l) milk
2 tablespoons of a tea of your choosing
2 cups coconut ice cream
1 lime peel
cane sugar or honey

1. Boil the milk.
2. Remove from heat and add tea. Cover and steep for 5 minutes.
3. Strain and let cool.
4. Chill in the refrigerator for a few hours.
5. In a blender, combine the ice cream, milk, tea and sweetener. Blend on high until smooth and creamy.
6. Add the lime peel.
7. Serve in tall glasses with a straw.

Korean tea

Ingredients:

4¼ cups (1 l) infusion Chinese or Korean tea
1 bag powdered ginseng
2 or 3 dried dates
pine nuts
cane sugar

1. Prepare an infusion with the tea, ginseng, and dates.
2. Sweeten to taste.
3. Serve with a few pine nuts in each cup or glass.

Cava with tea

Ingredients:

2 cups (½ l) Oolong tea
juice of one lemon
1 bottle cava
cane sugar

1. Mix the Oolong tea with lemon juice and sugar to taste.
2. Let chill for two or three hours in the fridge.
3. Mix in a jar with the cava and serve in champagne flutes

Tea grog

Ingredients:

2 cups (½ l) strong black tea
juice 3 lemons and 6 oranges
2 cups (½ l) curaçao and 2 cups (½ l) Burgundy wine
cane sugar

1. Prepare the tea and add the lemon and orange juices.
2. Sweeten to taste (4 cups of grog can have up to 250 g of sugar)
3. Add the curaçao and Burgundy and bring the whole mixture to a boil.
4. Remove from heat and serve in mugs.

Variation: "Shalimar tea" (alcohol-free)

1. Prepare the tea.
2. Put a slice of orange in the bottom of each glass and pour the tea while boiling (does not contain lemon, wine, or liquor).
3. Sweeten to taste.

Persian-style tea

Ingredients:

4¼ cups (1 l) milk
2 level tablespoons black tea
cane sugar or honey

1. Put the dry tea in a saucepan.
2. Boil milk and then pour over the tea.
3. Let steep for 5 minutes.
4. Sweeten to taste and serve.

Refreshing mint drink

Prepare the mint essence by boiling water with sugar for about 20 minutes, then add a few handfuls of mint and let simmer another 10 minutes, until the mixture thickens. Whenever you are thirsty, add a spoonful of this mixture to a glass of cold water and enjoy. It's said that Scheherazade, the beautiful storyteller, spun her tales of *A Thousand and One Nights* over a cup of mint tea—a notable aphrodisiac and cure for stress, headaches, and nerves.

Cooking with tea

Vegetable soup with green tea

Ingredients:
6 cups (1½ l) water
3 bags green tea
5 shiitake mushrooms, diced
1 red pepper, chopped
7 oz (200 g) celery, chopped
7 oz (200 g) cabbage, chopped
3 teaspoons miso
¼ teaspoon chili powder
3 spring onions

1. Boil water with the teabags.
2. Add the mushrooms, pepper, celery and cabbage. Bring to a boil again.
3. Cover and let simmer for five minutes, or until the vegetables are cooked.
4. Remove the tea bags and set aside a cup of the broth.
5. Mix the miso with this cup of hot broth and stir well. Pour it back into the soup, along with the chili powder and onions.
6. Simmer for a few more minutes and serve hot.

Vegetable soup with green tea

**Roasted peppers and potatoes,
with green tea and basil dressing**

Roasted peppers and potatoes, with green tea and basil dressing

Ingredients:
2.2 lbs (1 kg) potatoes
1 red pepper
1 yellow pepper
1 green pepper

For the dressing:
1 clove garlic
1 chili pepper
sea salt
1 spring onion
3 tablespoons olive oil
1 small cup green tea
5 fresh basil leaves
0.9 oz (25 g) used green tea leaves
1 teaspoon honey
1 tablespoon apple cider vinegar

1. Preheat the oven to 350°F (180°C). Bake the potatoes and whole peppers, turning occasionally, until cooked.
2. Meanwhile, prepare the dressing: grind the garlic, chili pepper, and a pinch of sea salt with a mortar and pestle to form a paste.
3. Cut the onion into thin slices (the white part and the tender part of the greens); cut the basil and tea leaves into thin strips.
4. In a bowl, combine all dressing ingredients and mix well.
5. Cut the potatoes and peppers in half and drizzle the dressing over top.

Tofu fajitas with green tea marinade

Ingredients:
For the marinade:
1¼ cups (300 ml) infusion green tea (reserve the used leaves)
¼ cup (50 ml) rice vinegar
Fresh ground black pepper
2 tablespoons apple extract
2 tablespoons extra virgin olive oil
2 tablespoons soy sauce

For the fajitas:
8.8 oz (250 g) grilled firm tofu
1 green pepper and ½ a red pepper
1 onion
2 tablespoons used green tea leaves
1 tablespoon sesame paste (tahini)
a few leaves lettuce, chopped
a handful soybean sprouts
3–4 corn tortillas

1. Strain the tea into a deep bowl, reserving the leaves for later use. Add the remaining ingredients for the marinade and mix.
2. Cut the tofu, peppers, and onion into strips. Place them in the marinade and let sit for an hour.
3. Sauté the marinated ingredients in a hot wok or frying pan with oil (with a little bit of marinade), on high heat and move continuously. Cut the green tea leaves into strips and add them to the pan.
4. Heat the tortillas in the oven, wrapped in aluminum foil, for 2–3 minutes. Spread a little tahini on the tortillas and fill them with lettuce, sprouts, and the fajita mixture. Serve immediately. This recipe can be altered to taste.

Tofu fajitas with green tea marinade

Green beans with tea marinade

Ingredients:
14 oz (400 g) green beans
2 cloves minced garlic
7 oz (200 g) sliced almonds
1 tablespoon canola oil
1.7 oz (50 g) black tea leaves boiled in 2 cups (500 ml) of water

1. Boil the green beans in a large pot of boiling water.
2. While the beans are boiling, sauté the garlic in a tablespoon of canola oil until opaque.
3. Add the tea infusion and simmer over a low heat with the garlic for a few minutes.
4. Remove the green beans from heat, drain, and place in a large bowl. Pour the tea marinade over the beans for one hour.
5. Strain the beans and sprinkle with sliced almonds and serve immediately.

Sauces

Spiced sesame sauce

For spring rolls

Ingredients:

0.9 oz (25 g) white sesame seeds

2 cloves garlic, peeled and finely chopped

1 spring onion, finely chopped

0.9 oz (25 g) boiled tea leaves, chopped

2 oz (60 g) teriyaki sauce

⅛ cup (30 ml) lemon juice

1 teaspoon sesame oil

1 teaspoon finely chopped chili pepper

1. Preheat the oven to 350°F (175°C). Toast the sesame seeds for 5 or 6 minutes, turning occasionally, until golden brown.

2. Place in a bowl and let cool.

3. Add the rest of the ingredients and grind in a blender or with a mortar and pestle.

4. Cover and let rest in the fridge for 30 minutes before using.

WHAT IS "CANOLA"?

The so-called "canola oil" is actually just rapeseed oil, given another name by producers after the public health crisis that rocked Spain two decades ago. "Canola" is a contraction of "Canada oil," for the country that started the commercialization of rapeseed oil. Natural canola—or rapeseed—oil has a lower saturated fat content than other vegetable oils, which makes it better for preventing cholesterol problems and heart disease.

Green tea ice cream

Desserts

Green tea ice cream

Ingredients:

4 bags green tea (removed from bags)
2 cups (500 ml) milk
4.4 oz (125 g) cane sugar
6 egg yolks
2 cups (500 ml) cream

1. Boil the milk with the green tea. Remove from heat and let sit for 5 minutes. Strain.
2. In a large bowl, beat the yolks and sugar until smooth. Add the warm milk. Bring two inches of water to a simmer in a medium saucepan, then set the bowl (with the yolks and sugar) over top. While stirring continuously, cook until it thickens. Remove from heat and continue stirring. Let cool.
3. Now is the time to add the cream and freeze it in the ice-cream maker. If you prefer to use the freezer, put the mixture in a metal bowl and store in the freezer for 3 or 4 hours. Then put in another container, and beat with a mixer until creamy and smooth. Return to the freezer, repeating the process twice more.
4. Finally, it's best to put into a serving dish, cover with plastic wrap, and store in the freezer until the following day.

Green tea with ice cream

1 cup fresh green tea
2 scoops vanilla ice cream (or preferred flavor)

1. This is a very simple recipe. Put the ice cream in a glass.
2. Pour the hot tea over top, forming a creamy liquid.

Green tea flan with vanilla and crunchy pistachio wafers

Ingredients:
for the flan:
4¼ cups (1 l) rice milk
½ vanilla bean
3 tablespoons agar-agar flakes
2 tablespoons green tea leaves
Honey to taste, as a sweetener

for the wafers:
3.5 oz (100 g) shelled and coarsely chopped pistachios
3.5 oz (100 g) cane sugar

for the sauce:
7 oz (200 g) shelled pistachios
1¼ cups (300 ml) rice milk
1 tablespoon cane sugar

1. Open the vanilla bean and scrape out the pulp with a knife. In a saucepan, boil the rice milk with the vanilla pulp and the agar-agar for 10 minutes. Grind the tea leaves to powder and add them; sweeten to taste and let cool.

2. Beat until the mixture becomes creamy, then pour into individual molds. Store in the fridge.

3. Prepare the crunchy wafers: in a small saucepan, heat the sugar over a low heat until it melts, add the pistachios, and mix well. Pour immediately over a sheet of waxed paper and cover with a second sheet. Flatten with a rolling pin and let solidify. Then cut it into irregular pieces.

4. To make the sauce, submerge the pistachios in boiling water for a few minutes, remove the skins, and beat with the almond milk until it is a uniform texture. Strain and set aside.

5. Remove the flan from the mold and serve with a drizzle of sauce and a crunchy wafer.

Green tea flan with vanilla and crunchy pistachio wafers

Summer tea with fruit

Ingredients:
2½ cups (600 ml) iced green tea
Ice cubes made from different fruit juices
Slices grapes, strawberries, pineapple, kiwi, apple, and orange

1. Put the ice cubes in tall glasses.
2. Pour the iced tea.
3. On long skewers, put a mixture of fruit slices and put one in each glass. In addition to decoration, you can eat the fruit as you drink the tea.

Green tea with cherries

Ingredients:
2½ cups (600 ml) iced green tea
6 oz (175 g) pitted cherries
1 slice fresh ginger, finely chopped
1 cinnamon stick
lemon juice
7 oz (200 g) raw sugar

1. Bring the cherries to a boil in two cups of the green tea and let simmer over a low heat for 15 minutes.
2. Boil the cinnamon and ginger in a separate pan with the remaining tea.
3. Pour the cherry mixture through a sieve and mix that liquid with the rest of the tea, cinnamon, and ginger.
4. Strain the mixture before adding the lemon juice and sugar. Serve cold.

Tea and mango sorbet

Ingredients:

⅝ cup (150 ml) green tea

3.5 oz (100 g) raw sugar

6 mangos, peeled and cubed

¾ cups (175 ml) fresh lime juice

1 slice ginger, peeled and chopped

    1. Boil the green tea with the sugar for five minutes. Let cool to room temperature.

    2. In a blender, prepare a puree of mango, lime juice, and ginger. Then, add the tea and sugar. Pour the mixture into a freezer safe container and freeze for 1 hour.

    3. Stir the sorbet occasionally while it is freezing to avoid ice crystals.

    4. After an hour, beat with a mixer and return to the freezer until it is ready to serve.

Therapeutic teas
Slimming Oolong

For diets and cleanses

Ingredients:
2 heaping tablespoons Oolong tea
3½ cups (850 ml) water

1. Preheat the teapot by filling it with warm water.
2. Heat the water in a saucepan and remove from heat just before it boils.
3. Empty the teapot and add the tea. Pour the water from the saucepan and let steep for 2 or 3 minutes. Let cool a little before drinking.

LOSE WEIGHT WITH TEA

Oolong tea is commonly used in weight-loss diets and has the additional advantage of containing very little theine. If you drink the above mixture two or three times a day, you will notice a gradual weight loss.

In the East, three-day cleanses based on tea, soup, fruits, and vegetables are common. The vegetables provide the necessary vitamins and nutrients, and the fruit helps clean the digestive system. Tea—and not just Pu-erh—helps with this kind of diet because it burns calories.

Tea with banana

Combats hypertension

Ingredients:

a few green tea leaves

1⅔ cups (400 ml) mineral water

1 slice banana, about an inch thick

1. Peel the slice of banana, crush in a mortar and pestle, and put in a mug.

2. Add the green tea leaves.

3. Bring the water to a boil and pour over the tea and banana.

4. Cover and let steep for 2 or 3 minutes.

FOR HIGH BLOOD PRESSURE

This recipe is great for hypertension, in which case it should be taken daily. Because of the strong smell and consistency of this fruit, it's best to prepare directly in a mug rather than a teapot, so the banana does not stick inside.

Burdock and sarsaparilla tea

Licorice tea

For irritated throats without cough

Ingredients:
Tea your choosing
6 or 7 slices dried licorice root

1. Put the slices of licorice in a teapot along with the tea leaves.
2. Boil the water and pour into the teapot.
3. Let steep for 5 minutes.

Burdock and sarsaparilla tea

An excellent cleansing cocktail to detox the body in the spring months

Ingredients:
1 oz (30 g) burdock root
1 oz (30 g) sarsaparilla root
0.35 oz (10 g) birch leaves
0.7 oz (20 g) dandelion

1. Combine all ingredients. Use one tablespoon of this mixture per glass of water, boil for 1 minute, and let steep for 10 minutes or more before straining and drinking.
2. This infusion should be taken three times a day, preferably before meals. To enhance its therapeutic effects, you can add a few drops of lemon juice.

Lemon balm and star anise tea

Honey and lemon tea

For irritated throats and coughs

Ingredients:
a few red Pu-erh tea leaves
½ organic lemon
honey

1. Cut the lemon in half and slice before putting it into the teapot.
2. Add the red tea leaves.
3. Boil the water and pour into the teapot.
4. Cover and wait until the drink is lukewarm. Add honey and serve.

Lemon balm and star anise tea

Effective anticellulite infusion

Ingredients:
1 oz (30 g) fucus algae
0.7 oz (20 g) star anise
0.7 oz (20 g) birch leaves
0.5 oz (15 g) verbena
0.5 oz (15 g) lemon balm leaves

1. Combine all ingredients. Put 2 tablespoons of the mixture in a pot with water and boil for 1 minute. Let steep for 10 minutes and strain.
2. This infusion should be drunk throughout the day, preferably a glass before every meal. In the summer it should be stored in the fridge.

Helps prevent water retention, which helps shed extra pounds.

Echinacea and plantain tea

Echinacea and plantain tea

To strengthen the immune system

Ingredients:

0.9 oz (25 g) echinacea

0.9 oz (25 g) plantain

0.9 oz (25 g) white pine needles

0.9 oz (25 g) coltsfoot

1. Heat water in a saucepan and remove from heat just before it boils.

2. Prepare the mixture in a teapot and add the hot water.

3. Let steep for 5 minutes, and then strain.

This is especially effective to fight colds and helps fortify the immune system. Take three times a day for three weeks. Rest for a week, then drink for three more weeks.

Sweet tea

For throat infections and gum sores

Ingredients:

a few green tea or Oolong leaves

raw sugar

1. Heat water in a saucepan and remove from heat just before it boils.

2. Put the tea in the teapot and add the water.

3. Add sugar and let steep for 2 or 3 minutes.

Lei Ch'a (ground tea)

For bouts of flu

Ingredients:

0.9 oz (25 g) green tea leaves
1.5 oz (45 g) long grain rice, uncooked
2 or 3 slices fresh ginger root
3½ cups (850 ml) water

1. Wash the rice and cut the ginger into thin slices.
2. Put the tea, rice, and ginger in a mortar with a little cold water and grind until it becomes a fine paste (can also be done in a blender).
3. Boil the water in a saucepan, add the paste, and let boil for a few minutes. Let cool before drinking.

Ginkgo, rosemary, mint, and summer savory tea

Ingredients:

0.7 oz (20 g) ginkgo
0.7 oz (20 g) rosemary
0.7 oz (20 g) mint
0.7 oz (20 g) summer savory

1. Mix all the ingredients
2. Boil the mixture in water for 30 seconds. Then let steep for 10 more minutes and strain. This infusion is best taken at mid-morning.

120

Ginkgo, rosemary, mint, and summer savory tea

Eucalyptus tea

Chrysanthemum tea

For treating sunstroke

Ingredients:

A few green tea leaves
20 white chrysanthemum flowers
3½ cups (850 ml) water

1. Wash the flowers and put in a saucepan.
2. Add the green tea.
3. Bring the water to a boil.
4. Pour and let steep for 2 or 3 minutes.

Eucalyptus tea

Ingredients:

9–10 eucalyptus leaves (2-3 per glass)
3½ cups (850 ml) water
Honey (preferably eucalyptus honey)

1. Bring the water to a boil and add the eucalyptus leaves.
2. Let the infusion steep for 10-12 minutes, and then sweeten with honey.

Eucalyptus (*Eucaliptus globulus*) is well known as an effective home remedy for colds, lung problems, and asthma attacks. Traditionally it is inhaled as a vapor. Taking this two or three times a day helps stop mucus and provides excellent results.

Tomato tea

For increasing appetite

Ingredients:

a few green tea leaves

1 tomato the size of a ping pong ball

raw sugar (optional)

1. Wash the tomato and cut into cubes without peeling.

2. Put the tomato and tea leaves in a saucepan.

3. Bring water to a boil and pour over top.

4. Add sugar if desired, cover, and let steep for 2 or 3 minutes.

Thyme and elder tea

Prevents and combats respiratory problems

Ingredients:

0.7 oz (20 g) thyme flowers

0.7 oz (20 g) elder flowers

0.7 oz (20 g) gentian root

0.7 oz (20 g) echinacea root

1. Combine all ingredients. Use 1 tablespoon of the mixture per cup and boil the combination for 1 minute. Then let steep for 10 minutes and strain.

You should drink a cup daily for three months: drinking it for three weeks and stopping for the fourth.

Thyme and elder tea

Chamomile, elecampane, pansy, and houseleek tea

Effective in combating allergy symptoms

Ingredients:

0.7 oz (20 g) chamomile flowers
1 oz (30 g) elecampane root
0.7 oz (20 g) wild pansy flower
1 oz (30 g) houseleek flower

1. Combine the ingredients in a saucepan along with water and boil for 2 minutes. Cover and let steep for another 10 minutes.
2. Strain and drink twice a day. Drink on alternating days for two weeks (drinking one day and resting the next) during the spring.

Rice vinegar tea

Alleviates intestinal pains

Ingredients:

a few green tea leaves
3 or 4 teaspoons white rice vinegar

1. Put the green tea in a saucepan.
2. Boil water and pour over the tea.
3. Add the vinegar and let steep for 2 or 3 minutes before drinking.

Chamomile, elecampane, pansy, and houseleek tea

Tea Life

Tea time tales

Tasseomancy: the future in the leaves

An inspiring cup

Flavor and good health

A brief dictionary of tea

Tea time tales

As we saw in the chapter on the Japanese tea ceremony, tea time is perfect for relaxed conversation with family or friends. But it can also be a great opportunity for solitude and seclusion, as the aroma and taste of the infusion revitalize us after a stressful day.

The ten traditional stories collected in this section invite tranquility and reflection. The tradition of telling stories at tea time is deeply rooted in China, where professional storytellers visit teahouses and offer a beautiful tale in exchange for a few coins.

The answers

A young Zen apprentice was on his way to the market to buy vegetables for the monastery, when he crossed paths with a student of another monastery.

"Where are you going?" the first student asked.

"Where my legs carry me," the other replied.

The first student reflected on this answer for a long time, since he was certain it contained a deep meaning. When he got back to the monastery, he described the conversation to his teacher, who replied:

"You should have asked what he would do if he did not have legs."

The next day, the student was excited to spot the same boy along the road. He approached him and said:

"Where are you going today? Where your legs carry you, I suppose. But let me ask you . . ."

The Fox and the Tiger

Once upon a time, there was a tiger who managed to capture a fox. When he was about to devour it, the fox, who was very clever, said to him:

"Stop, you fool! Don't you see that I'm the king of all the jungle animals. No matter how strong you are, you can't harm me. What's more, the God of the Sky will punish you cruelly if you don't submit to me."

"What are you saying?" the tiger exclaimed, laughing. "You, the king of the jungle. You'll have to prove it if you don't want me to wolf you down whole."

"Easy," the fox replied with an arrogant confidence. "Let's go into the jungle. Follow me closely and you'll see how all the animals are afraid of me."

With a proud, steady step, the fox entered the jungle, followed closely behind by the tiger. The tiger was astonished to see how all the animals fled from the fox, without realizing that it was actually the tiger himself that they feared. Impressed by the demonstration, the tiger bowed before the fox and recognized him as the king of the jungle.

The Silence

In a temple in the remote mountains of Japan, four Zen monks decided to take a retreat that demanded absolute silence. It was very cold, and when a gust of icy wind came into the temple, the youngest monk exclaimed:

"The candle went out!"

"Why are you talking?" the oldest monk scolded him. "We are doing a silent meditation."

"Why are you both talking instead of shutting your mouths as we agreed?" the third monk shouted, indignant.

"I'm the only one who isn't talking here," the fourth monk said smugly.

The Rich and the Poor

Once upon a time, in China, there was a very wealthy man, accustomed to the respect and praise of everyone around him. But there was one exception: an extremely poor man who had never given him any praise, which confused the powerful gentleman.

One day, he ordered his servants to bring the miserable man to his presence and decided to tempt him:

"If I give you a quarter of my wealth, will you flatter me?"

"That distribution would be too unequal to earn my praise," the poor man replied soberly.

"And if I gave you half? Would you praise me if you had half my fortune?"

"In that case, we'd both have the same and there'd be no reason for flattery."

Desperate, the rich man made one last offer:

"And if I gave you all my riches? What would you do?"

"If I had such a large fortune, why would I praise you?"

The Flag and the Wind

A Zen master was coming back from his morning walk when, in the monastery entrance, he found two monks arguing in front of a flag with the image of Buddha, waving in the wind.

"It's the flag that is moving," one shouted.

"No, it's the wind that is moving," the other replied heatedly.

"You are completely wrong."

"You are looking at the consequence, not the cause."

The argument became so heated that it was about to come to blows, but then they saw that their master had arrived, and they both asked in unison:

"Master, which is moving, the flag or the wind?"

"Neither one," he concluded, "It's your minds that are moving."

The Man on the Hill

Three friends had gone for a hike through the beautiful, gently rolling hills, when they spotted a man sitting alone on a hillside.

"He must be lost and waiting for someone to pass by to help him," one of the friends declared.

"I don't think so," another said. "It seems like he's not feeling well and sat down to rest."

"You're both wrong," the third said. "Obviously he's waiting for a friend to meet up with him."

While they walked toward the stranger, the three friends began to argue over which of them was correct, rejecting the arguments of the other two. When they reached the hillside, they decided to ask the man to see who was right.

"Are you lost?" one asked.

"No," the man replied.

"Are you sick?" another asked.

"No," the stranger said again.

"Are you waiting for someone?" the third asked.

"No," he replied again.

Confused, the three friends asked together, "So what are you doing here?"

The stranger smiled and said calmly, "I simply am being."

The Sentence

After the death of a wealthy man, his two sons began to fight bitterly over the division of the inheritance. After many lawsuits, the judges divided the inheritance, but neither of the sons was content.

Since they were at the point of starting litigation over again, the tribunal decided to take the difficult decision to the emperor himself, whose verdict would finally put an end to the brothers' quarrel.

One of the emperor's ministers, celebrated for his wisdom, offered to resolve the case with the emperor's permission. The minister called the two brothers together, and both complained bitterly about the unjust distribution. In light of this, the minister asked each party to sign a document swearing that what they had said was completely true.

The brothers agreed with this request readily. With the signed documents in hand, the minister delivered his sentence immediately.

"Since you both accuse each other of having received more inheritance, I order you both to trade your possessions at once."

The Beginning and the End

A Zen apprentice accidentally broke a valuable vase that belonged to his teacher. When he saw the teacher approaching, he gathered up the pieces of the vase and hid them in his robe.

When the teacher came in, the student asked him: "Why do we die, teacher?"

"It is natural," he replied. "Everything has a beginning and an end. Everything should live the time it is meant to and no more. Then it should die."

So the student let the broken pieces fall to the floor. "Then it was your vase's time to die, teacher."

The Funeral Ode

In a small town, the mother of a farmer died, and he ran to the house of a teacher to ask him to write a funeral ode for the burial, as was the custom at the time. The teacher accepted the task and told the farmer that he would have it finished the next day.

Since he had never been asked such a thing before, the teacher looked in an old book that had a funeral ode dedicated to the father of a family, and copied it word for word. The next day, he gave it to the farmer without accepting any payment.

An hour later, the man came running back to the teacher's house and said: "Teacher, a friend of mine who can read told me this ode is wrong."

"What's wrong with it?" the teacher asked angrily. "I copied it word for word from a book. I'm certain I did not make a single error. The thing is, in your family your mother died wrongly; it should have been your father."

Tasseomancy:
the future in the leaves

Tasseomancy is the art of reading the future in tea leaves. This form of divination originated in ancient China, although it became rather popular in Europe during the eighteenth and nineteenth centuries. To practice, you must use a traditional infusion of loose tea leaves, since tea bags don't leave dregs.

Preparation

In a white or light-colored cup, measure one or two teaspoons of tea, preferably black tea, and pour hot water over it. Do not use a strainer. The consultant—the person who is going to read the fortune—should drink the tea, leaving a little liquid and the tea leaves in the bottom of the cup.

Next, swirl the leaves in a circle three times and turn the cup upside down over a plate. Tap the bottom three times to unstick most of the leaves. Then remove the cup to begin interpreting.

Interpretation

The reading is done using the shapes and figures formed by the leaves stuck on the inside of the cup. You will often see lines and geometric shapes that form more complex images such as objects, plants, and animals.

Traditionally, the reading is done clockwise around the cup, starting at the handle. The figures that appear near the handle represent recent events or events that are about to occur. The symbols on the bottom of the cup represent the current emotions of the reader. Those found near the rim usually describe coming events related to love or friendship.

This small dictionary indicates the meaning of common symbols. However, this is only a starting point to completing a personalized reading, which takes into account the situation and the reader's character:

Anchor: Your projects will be delayed for a time.

Arrow: If it's pointing upward it means your luck will improve; if it points downward, you will have to wait.

Bag: You will receive an unexpected gift.

Balloon: Possibility of a long journey.

Banana: A good time to bring all types of business to terms.

Bat: Without realizing, you've gotten into something dark.

Bed: You will have a period of emotional well-being.

Bee: You will be repaid for efforts made.

Bell: News from an old friend you haven't seen in a while.

Bird: Good ideas; traveling soon.

Bone: Take extreme precautions; risk of accident.

Book: Time of great discoveries; intellectual progress.

Branch: A new friendship will enrich your life.

Butterfly: Leaving behind projects and people that weren't giving you anything.

Cake: You will be invited to a party soon.

Cane: You need to find support for future undertakings.

Car: You will be offered a new job.

Cat: You should be very alert; a tricky situation will require great agility on your part.

Chair: An unexpected guest will appear.

Circle: If the circle is complete, you will finish a project; if it's broken, there will be delays.

Clock: Time runs out; you will have to act.

Clouds: You will pass through a period of great doubt.

Compass: There will be a sudden change of direction in your life.

Coin: Someone will call on you to repay a debt.

Crab: A setback in plans that seemed promising.

Crocodile: Warning about approaching dangers.

Cross: You will encounter an obstacle in your path.

Cup: You will have to take on new responsibilities.

Diamond: You will receive a valuable gift; discoveries.

Dog: A friend will support you in a new project.

Donkey: Upcoming difficulties will require all of your patience.

Dragon: Big changes will give your life a new meaning.

Drum: You will hear from someone you lost touch with.

Duck: You will receive an unexpected invitation.

Ear: Surprising information will change the course of your life.

Egg: An important transformation is ahead; new perspectives.

Envelope: News from abroad; you may receive money unexpectedly.

Eye: A crisis is coming that will require great vigilance.

Face: A new person will have a big impact on your life.

Feather: A great coincidence is imminent; time to reflect.

Fish: You will begin a spiritual search.

Fist: A betrayal is coming; you should be alert.

Flag: Soon you will face a danger; vigilance recommended.

Flowers: An ex-lover will make a reappearance.

Frog: You will have a stroke of good luck.

Glass: New experiences on the horizon; you should be open to them.

Glove: A complicated situation will require a lot of tact.

Goat: You are about to do something reckless; check yourself.

Grape: Effort invested will soon bear fruit.

Guitar: Happiness is in view; new friends will join your group.

Hammer: You will have to fight against adversity.

Hand: A friend needs your help urgently.

Hat: You will be offered a new job that requires travel.

Horn: A time of abundance; it is time to share.

Horseshoe: Luck is on your side; now is the time to take risks.

An inspiring cup

Many have spoken of the virtues and spirit of this mythical infusion. In the eighth century of this age, the venerable master of tea Lu Yu wrote the first book on the subject: *Cha Ching*, the Book of Tea.

In this chapter we offer a selection of the best quotes and adages about the fragrant world of tea, from some of the all-time greatest poets as well as rock stars like Mick Jagger and diverse characters such as Agatha Christie and Woody Allen. Recommended reading with a warm cup in hand.

Health and longevity

Tea is a cup of life.
    ANONYMOUS

Drink a cup of tea a day
and the pharmacist will die of hunger.
CHINESE PROVERB

The best thing about tea, above all else,
is that it keeps the gray matter going.
    ANONYMOUS

If you're cold, tea will warm you.
If you're hot, it will refresh you.
If you're anxious, it will calm you.
   WILLIAM GLADSTONE

Good tea motivates the idle,
relaxes the studious, and dilutes the meals
of those who don't exercise.
   SAMUEL JOHNSON

I adore tea. It is my elixir of eternal youth.
Physical and mental youth.
   REGINA HELKER

Where there's tea, there's hope.
   ARTHUR PINERO

Tea is a magical product,
perhaps even the eighth wonder of the world.
   H. RAHMAN

Preparation

No one can teach you to prepare the perfect cup of tea.
It's simply something that happens now and then.
Of course, wearing wool always helps.
   JILL DUPLEX

The perfect temperature for tea
is two degrees below necessary.
   TERRI GUILLEMETS

The best tea in the world is prepared
by the student at Oxford or Cambridge,
for whom it is as important as tobacco.
They lean over the teapot with the air
of Roger Bacon in his laboratory.
    E. V. Lucas

Tea and water give life to each other, the professor said.
Tea is still alive. This tea has tea, and also the vitality of water, he added.
    Jason Goodwin

My tea time is four thirty
and my buttered toast waits for no one.
    Wilkie Collins

Tea without milk is not a civilized drink.
    Colin Blythe

Women are like tea bags.
You don't know how strong they are until they're in hot water.
    Eleanor Roosevelt

Morning tea brings with it a joy
that afternoon or evening tea cannot match.
    Oliver Wendell Holmes

Love and scandal are the best sweeteners for tea.
    Henry Fielding

The quality of tea is a decision
that belongs to the mouth.
    Lu Yu

The best tea leaves should have creases
like the leather boots of the horsemen from Tartar,
roll like the skin that hangs from the neck of a powerful ox,
unfold like the mist that comes up from the valley,
shine like a lake touched by wind, and finally,
be damp and sweet to the touch like earth newly washed with rain.
    Lu Yu

The matrons swirl the cup
and see the future in the leaves.
    Alexander Pope

I got nasty habits.
I take tea at three.
    Mick Jagger

Calm

Drink tea to forget the constant turmoil of the world.
    Tien Yiheng

Remember the tea kettle:
he's always up to his neck in hot water
and he still whistles!
    Anonymous

Tea revives our imaginations.
It represses the vapors that invade the head
and keeps the soul's palace calm.
    Edmund Waller

Few moments in life are as pleasant
as that dedicated to the afternoon tea ceremony.
HENRY JAMES

It's strange how a teapot can embody both
the pleasure of solitude and that of company.
ANONYMOUS

I'm an unrepentant and shameless tea drinker.
For twenty years I have diluted my meals exclusively
with the infusion of this fascinating plant.
With tea I have livened the afternoon, with tea I have enjoyed my nights,
and with tea I have welcomed the mornings.
SAMUEL JOHNSON

There is no problem so grave that cannot be much diminished
by a nice cup of tea.
BERNARD-PAUL HEROUX

Drink your tea slowly and reverently,
as if it were the axle that makes the world turn:
slowly, serenely,
without rushing into the future.
THICH NHAT HANH

The mere clinking of cups and saucers
induces a happy calm on the mind.
GEORGE GISSING

For the English, tea
really is an indoors picnic.
ALICE WALKER

An inspiring cup

151

Conversation and tea are his specialty, said Giles.
He's just come in… let's see if tea and buns
can make the world a better place.
    AGATHA CHRISTIE

I can never find a cup of tea big enough
or a book long enough to suit me.
    C.S. LEWIS

I hope the next time we meet
we don't have to fight each other.
Instead we'll be drinking a cup of tea.
    JACKIE CHAN

Make tea, not war.
    MONTY PYTHON

Tea time is a resort for the soul.
You leave behind your worries and work.
Busy people forget their tasks.
Your stress dissolves, your feelings awaken…
    ALEXANDRA STODDARD

The spirit of tea is
calm, well being, and refinement.
    ARTHUR GRAY

Theism is a cult founded from adoration
of beauty among the sordid facts of daily existence.
It instills in us purity and harmony, the mystery of charity,
the romanticism of the social order.
    OKAKURA KAKUZO

Tea is the favorite drink of intellectuals.
Thomas de Quincy

Perhaps that is the true gift of a teatime celebration:
It fills our cups with joy and warmth and friendship.
May the echo of the teacups' message be heard not only at Christmas,
not only on special occasions,
but anytime friends come together.
Emilie Barnes

What is the most marvelous thing for people who,
like me, follow the way of the tea?
My answer: the unity between host and guest
that is created heart to heart when they share
a cup of tea… you feel as one with nature
and you find peace.
Soshitsu Sen

Poetry

There is much poetry and delicate feelings
in a tin of tea.
Ralph Waldo Emerson

Each cup of tea represents an imaginary journey.
Catherine Douzel

I have always feared that creation will end
before tea time.
Sidney Smith

Flavor and good health

Here we present a summary of a text by Kenneth S. Cohen, renowned master of qigong, scholar of Chinese culture, and specialist in matters of health. Cohen, who began his studies in 1969, is fluent in Chinese, and well-versed in taoism, collaborated with Alan Watts and worked alongside the greatest master of tea to write this text. He was one of the pioneers in introducing qigong to the West and establishing a link between qigong and medicine. We recommend his book, which is a real treasure for health, *The Way of Qigong*.

Pour yourself a cup of tea!

The classic texts on Chinese herbal medicine usually include a few paragraphs on ginseng, but the commentary on tea takes up various chapters. In China, almost all the experts on manipulation of qi, or energy, (acupuncturists, calligraphers, practitioners of martial arts, and qigong), drink tea regularly. Here are some of their motives:

Tea is as ancient as medicine in China. More than two thousand years ago, the legendary Divine Farmer (*Shen Neng*), catalogued all the medicinal plants in China. He personally tried each plant, drinking a cup of tea after each to neutralize any possible toxicity. (Don't try this at home; it only works for divine farmers). He felt the effect of each plant on his qi and documented it in the first edition of *Shen Neng Ben Cao Jing (Classic Medicinal Plants of Shen Neng)*.

One of the most powerful anti-carcinogens is epigallocatechin gallate (EGCG). Since the process of toasting and fermenting destroys most of the EGCG, this is only found in high concentrations in green tea.

Tea strengthens the immune system and is antibacterial. In ancient China, powdered green tea or chewed leaves were applied as an external poultice to stop infections in wounds or insect stings. Powdered tea can inhibit the growth of staphylococcus, salmonella, and other dangerous germs. Tea can also kill bacteria in the mouth, which helps prevent cavities. The natural fluoride in tea strengthens enamel.

The antioxidant properties of tea are key to understanding its many benefits, such as the traditional link between tea and longevity. *Antioxidants* destroy or deactivate free radicals, which basically affect our body the way oxygen affects oils: it makes them old and rancid.

Therefore antioxidant-rich foods, such as tea, keep us fresh and young.

Tea is also rich in nutrients, although the quantity contained in each cup is naturally rather small. It contains insoluble vitamin A (80mg/100g) and chlorophyll (3 percent), which aren't useful to us if the tea leaves have been soaked, and small

Tea bags

This practical invention came to us courtesy of Thomas Sullivan, a businessman from New York who, in 1904, decided to give up selling loose tea in cans in favor of small handmade silk bags. His customers discovered that they didn't need to remove the tea from the bags, but rather could just pour the water directly over them. In this way, they avoided the cumbersome step of straining the tea. He began to sell tea in little bags, and it was an instant success because it was so practical. However, there are some disadvantages.

Tea bags contain ground leaves that are often of lower quality than loose tea. Until now, black tea was the most commonly sold in bags, although lately green tea, often flavored with mint, is gaining popularity.

It is also important to keep in mind that the material used to make each bag should be biodegradable and unbleached.

quantities of vitamins B1, B2, niacin, and folic acid. There's enough magnesium and iodine to account for the observed antacid effects of tea. It is very rich in vitamin C (250 mcg/100g), although black tea loses some of this during fermentation. A normal cup of green tea (about a teaspoon of tea leaves) will release about six milligrams of vitamin C on its third use. A cup of black tea contains about 58 mg of potassium.

And caffeine? The caffeine in coffee puts the nerves on edge. Some people say it gives them a "boost." I say it gives "anxiety." Coffee prepares you for war. The Institute of Medicine of the US National Academy of Sciences has recommended adding caffeine to the food rations given to soldiers. Maybe they should substitute it with tea! If soldiers drank tea, they would probably be in a more meditative and conscious state, ready to act but not pushed to do so. These qualities are highly esteemed in Japanese and Chinese martial arts. One possible explanation for the different effects of coffee and tea is that although they both contain caffeine, tea contains other substances that alter or mitigate the effect of caffeine. Coffee also contains significantly more caffeine than tea does.

Keep in mind, you should always take precautions, even when using this marvelous drug. Never drink tea that was made the day before and left in the cup or teapot. Tea should be freshly made in order to enjoy its healing effects. You may need to reduce your tea intake if you suffer from insomnia, arrhythmia, or are pregnant. And remember that any beverage that contains caffeine can negatively interact with birth control pills, ulcer medications, tranquilizers, or antidepressants that are monoamine oxidase inhibitors.

A brief dictionary of tea

agony of the leaves: expression describing the moment that the tea leaves unfold from the effect of the heat.

Anhui: one of the largest tea-producing regions of China.

aroma: fragrance that the tea leaves release that comes from the essential oils.

Assam: region in the northeast of India where *Camellia assamica* (the basis of black tea, offers a strong flavor and dark-colored infusion) is grown; this type of tea is also harvested in Darjeeling.

astringency: the sensation of dryness in the mouth produced by teas with unoxidized polyphenols.

autumnal: name given to teas that are harvested in autumn.

Bancha: variety of green tea with low theine content; the most common in Japan.

bergamot: essential oil of the bergamot orange, used to flavor teas such as Earl Grey.

black: the most widely consumed tea in the West; prepared from green tea leaves that are oxidized—or fermented—to obtain a reddish infusion.

blend: mixture of teas from different sources to obtain a more consistent taste.

blue: name given to semi-fermented teas, halfway between green and black teas; also called Oolong.

body: term used by the masters of tea to refer to the consistency of the infusion.

catechins: class of polyphenol present in high concentrations in green tea, and in lower quantities in other derivative teas.

Ceilan: colonial name of modern-day Sri Lanka; denomination of the teas produced in this island south of India.

cha: Romanized spelling of the word *tea* in Chinese and Japanese.

chai: name given to tea in India; masala chai (mixed tea) is a strong infusion based on black tea and spices, normally served with milk and sugar.

Chum mee: a popular tea in China, whose long, fine leaves look like little eyebrows; produces a mild, pale yellow infusion.

Congou: name given to black tea from China; derived from the original name, *gongfu*.

Darjeeling: region in the northeast of India that gives its name to the tea grown there; these plantations in the Himalayas produce what is considered the champagne of teas, mainly black teas.

Earl Grey: black tea flavored with oil of bergamot.

English breakfast: strong black tea consumed mainly in Great Britain to wake up in the morning.

fermentation: process used to make black tea and Oolong; this process helps the natural enzymes in the tea to oxidize the green leaf and give it the characteristic color and aroma.

first flush: variety made from the first buds of spring.

flavored: mixtures that are usually made with a base of low-quality tea, with fruit, flowers, spices, or essential oils added.

Formosa: teas produced in Taiwan, primarily Oolong.

Genmaicha: green tea with toasted rice; frequently consumed by the Japanese with meals.

green: dried, unfermented tea leaves; consumed mainly in China and Japan.

ground: tea cut into pieces in a food processor; no leaves or buds are left whole.

Gunpowder: popular green tea from China whose leaves are compressed into little balls; they open up on contact with hot water.

Gyokuro: Japanese green tea obtained from plants that grow in the shade; also called Pearl Dew.

jasmine: black tea flavored with jasmine, very popular in China; typically made from the Pouchong variety of black tea.

Keemum: the highest quality black tea grown in central China; normally it is rolled and toasted by hand.

Kenya: one of the fullest bodied black teas; in the African country it is often sold in a powdered form, similar to coffee.

Kokeicha: Japanese green tea, powdered and pressed into fine needles; produces a yellowish infusion with a pronounced taste.

Lady Grey: fruity version of Earl Grey, with orange peel and rose petals.

Lapsang souchong: Chinese black tea dried over a pine wood fire to give a characteristic smoky taste.

Lung ching: in Chinese, "dragonwell;" green tea from the Hangzhou region, celebrated for its emerald color and sweet taste.

Matcha: powdered green tea that is used in the Japanese tea ceremony; produces a rich, astringent, jade-colored infusion.

Oolong: variety of tea characterized by its large leaves and light taste of the infusion; it is lightly fermented, halfway between green and black tea; also known as blue tea.

Orange pekoe: does not refer to the quality or the taste, but rather the size of the leaves; this name indicates the maximum size of whole tea leaves.

Pai mu tan: the most well-known variety of white tea, with prodigious healing properties.

polyphenols: natural astringents present in tea.

powder: the finest tea, normally associated with a lower quality; the kind used in commercial tea bags.

Pu-erh: popularly known as red tea, variety from the Yunnan province of China known for its weight loss power; made from wet green tea that is fermented microbiologically to darken it.

rain tea: leaves harvested during the rainy season.

red: name given to Pu-erh; in South Africa the same name is given to the national infusion, Rooibos.

Samovar: very popular mixture in Russia made from Chinese black tea with a light smoky touch.

second flush: tea made from the leaves and buds that grow after the monsoon rains.

Sencha: Japanese green tea similar to Bacha, but better quality.

smoked: tea leaves that have been dried over a wood fire to give them a characteristic taste.

Souchong: name used in China to refer to the big leaves harvested from the third or fourth shoot of the plant.

Sumatra: black tea with an intense flavor that is grown on the Indonesian island of the same name.

theine: synonym for caffeine; a stimulating compound present in tea.

Ti kuan yin: literally "Iron Goddess of Mercy;" variety of Oolong that ferments for more time and acquires darker color and more intense flavor.

Tip: also called tippy; tea with a high content of young buds.

tisane: infusion of other plants.

white: special variety of green tea that is distinguished by the presence of white filaments in the buds, and a much clearer infusion.

yellow: variety of mature, unfermented tea; takes its name from the color of the infusion.

Yunnan: region in the southeast of China that produces black teas with spiced flavors, in addition to the famous Pu-erh.

Recipes index

Selected Bibliography

BAGCHI, DEBASIS, *Green Tea: Antioxidant Power to Fight Disease*, McGraw-Hill, 1999

BARNES, EMILIE, *If Teacups Could Talk*, Harvest House, 1994

BROCHARD, GILLES, *The Book of Tea*, Olañeta, 1998

BRUNEL, HENRI, *Los Más Bellos Cuentos Zen* (*The Most Beautiful Zen Stories*), Olañeta, 2003

CHANG, YING & OTHERS, *Cooking with Green Tea*, Putnam, 2000

CHOW, KIT & KRAMER, *All the Tea in China*, China Books and Periodicals, 1990

COHEN, KENNETH, *El Camino del Qigong* (*The Way of Qigong*), La Liebre de Marzo, 2004

DOLBY, VICTORIA, *All About Green Tea*, Putnam, 1998

FARRELL, MARY E., *From Cha to Tea: a study of the influence of tea drinking on British culture*, Publicacions De L'uji, 2002

FERMINE, MAXENCE, *Opium*, Anagrama, 2003

Goodwin, Jason, *The Gunpowder Gardens*, Vintage, 1993

Gustafson, Helen, *The Green Tea User's Manual*, Clarkson N. Potter, 2001

Hara, Yukihiko, *Green Tea Health Benefits and Applications*, Marcel Dekker, 2001

Harrer, Heinrich, *Seven Years in Tibet*, Juventud, 1987

Huete, Anna, *Energía para Beber* (*Energy to Drink*), Ed. Océano Ámbar, 2005

Isobuchi, Takeshi, *Searching for Tea*, Japan, 1994

Jumeau-Laford, Jacques, *Le The*, Nathan, 1988

Kakuzo, Okakura, *The Book of Tea*, Tuttle, 2000. Edition in Spanish: ed. Kairós. Edition in Catalan: ed. Altafulla

Kam Chuen, Lam, *The Way of Tea*, Gaia, 2002

Man-Tu Lee, Anthony, *The Japanese Tea Ceremony*, Element, 1999

Maxwell, Fernando, *The Geography of Tea*, Standard T.C., 2001

Mellor, Isha, *The Little Tea Book*, Olañeta, 1986

Mitscher, Lester, *The Green Tea Book*, Putnam, 1997

Oppliger, Peter, *Green Tea*, C.W. Daniel, 1998

Podreka, Tomislav, *Serendipitea*, William Morrow & Co., 1998

Pratt, James Norwood, *Tea Lovers Treasury*, Cole Group, 1995

Pruess, Joanna, *Eat Tea*, The Lyons Press, 2001

Purti, Iona & Arturo Marcelo Pascual, *Green Tea and other Revitalizing Tisanes*, Ed. Océano Ámbar, 2003

Purtí, Iona & Rodolfo Román, *Té Pu-erh y Rooibos* (*Pu-erh and Rooibos Teas*), Ed. Océano Ámbar, 2004

Rasmussen, Wendy & Ric Rhinehart, *Tea Basics*, John Wiley & Sons, 1999

Roselló, Dr. Ramon, *El Sano Placer de Las Tisanas* (*The Healthy Pleasure of Tea*), Ed. RBA Integral, 1998

Rosen, Diana, *Green Tea*, Vermont, 1998

Sen, Shohitsu, *The Japanese Way of Tea*, University of Hawaii Press, 1998

Shiru, Chang & Ramiro Calle, *101 Cuentos Clásicos de la China* (*101 Classic Tales from China*), Edaf, 2002

Taylor, Nadine, *Green Tea*, Obelisco, 2000

Tekulsky, Mathew, *Making Your Own Gourmet Tea Drinks*, Crown, 1995

Udall, Kate Gilbert, *Green Tea: Fight Cancer, Lower Cholesterol, Live Longer*, Woodland, 1998

Yamamoto, Takehiko, *Chemistry and Applications of Green Tea*, CRC Press, 1997

Yi, Sabine & Others, *El Libro del Amante del Té (The Tea Lover's Book)*, Olañeta, 1986

Zak, Victoria, *20,000 Secrets of Tea*, Dell Pub, 1999

Zittlau, Jorg, *Green Tea for Health & Vitality*, Putnam, 1998